RAIN FORESTS
TROPICAL TREASURES

Other Titles in *Ranger Rick's NatureScope*

Ranger Rick's NatureScope

RAIN FORESTS
TROPICAL TREASURES

National Wildlife Federation

LEARNING TRIANGLE PRESS

Connecting kids, parents, and teachers through learning

An imprint of McGraw-Hill

New York San Francisco Washington, D.C. Auckland Bogotá Caracas
Lisbon London Madrid Mexico City Milan Montreal New Delhi
San Juan Singapore Sydney Tokyo Toronto

Library of Congress Cataloging-in-Publication Data applied for

McGraw-Hill

A Division of The **McGraw·Hill** *Companies*

NATIONAL WILDLIFE FEDERATION®

1 2 3 4 5 6 7 8 9 JDL/JDL 9 0 2 1 0 9 8 7

ISBN 0-07-046510-X

NatureScope® was originally conceived by National Wildlife Federation's School Programs Editorial Staff, under the direction of Judy Braus, Editor. Special thanks to all of the Editorial Staff, Scientific, Educational Consultants and Contributors who brought this series of eighteen publications to life.

NATIONAL WILDLIFE FEDERATION EDITORIAL STAFF
Creative Services Manager: Sharon Schiliro
Editor, Ranger Rick® magazine: Gerry Bishop
Director Classroom–related Programs: Margaret Tunstall
Contributors: Carol Boggis, Rhonda Lucas Donald, Sharon Levy, Susan Makurat–Bond

McGRAW-HILL EDP STAFF
Acquisitions Editor: Judith Terrill-Breuer
Editorial Supervisor: Patricia V. Amoroso
Production Supervisor: Claire Stanley
Designer: Jaclyn J. Boone
Cover Design: David Saylor

MEETING THE CHALLENGE

GOAL

Ranger Rick's Nature-Scope is a creative education series dedicated to inspiring in children an understanding and appreciation of the natural world while developing the skills they will need to make responsible decisions about the environment.

It has been almost a decade since publication of the first *Rain Forests: Tropical Treasures* in the **Ranger Rick's NatureScope** series. Since that time, we have had both encouraging and discouraging news about the environment. Our awareness has been heightened and much has been done, but there is still much to do.

One of the best ways to ensure sustained concern for our planet and the creatures who inhabit it is to educate our children. This new edition of *Rain Forests: Tropical Treasures* brings to the classroom the original material which has survived the test of time, along with new essays by and about people working in the field today, people who are still learning about how our environment works and who are taking action to preserve it. Here also is the sense of wonder they feel as they work in the natural world. This new edition also includes an updated bibliography for further study and enrichment.

The effort to save wildlife and habitat will span many generations. Like all lifelong commitments, there is no better time to begin than when we are young.

National Wildlife Federation

TABLE OF CONTENTS

Rain Forests
Tropical Treasures

A CLOSE-UP LOOK AT RAIN FORESTS: TROPICAL TREASURES

L ooking at the Table of Contents, you can see we've divided *Rain For ests: Tropical Treasures* into four chapters (each of which deals with a broad tropical rain forest theme), a craft section, and an appendix. Each chapter includes *background information* that explains concepts and vocabulary, *activities* that relate to the chapter theme, and *Copycat Pages* that reinforce many of the concepts introduced in the activities.

You can choose single activity ideas or teach each chapter as a unit. Either way, each activity stands by itself and includes teaching objectives, a list of materials needed, suggested age groups, subjects covered, and a step-by-step explanation of how to do the activity. (The objectives, materials, age groups, and subjects are highlighted in the left-hand margin for easy reference.) Outdoor activities are coded with this symbol:

AGE GROUPS
The suggested age groups are:
- Primary (grades K–2)
- Intermediate (grades 3–5)
- Advanced (grades 6–8)

Each chapter begins with primary activities and ends with intermediate or ad vanced activities. But don't feel bound by the grade levels we suggest. You'll be able to adapt many of the activities to fit your particular age group and needs.

COPYCAT PAGES
The *Copycat Pages* supplement the activities and include ready-to-copy maps, puzzles, coloring pages, and worksheets. Look at the bottom of each Copycat Page for the name and page number of the activity that it goes with. *Answers to a Copycat Pages are in the texts of the activities.*

WHAT'S AT THE END
The fifth section, *Crafty Corner*, will give you some art and craft ideas that com plement many of the activities in the first four chapters. And the last section, the *Appendix*, is loaded with reference suggestions that include books, films, and posters. The *Appendix* also has a glossary and a list of rain forest exhibits around the country.

An Overview

Two hundred years ago, tropical rain forests circled the globe in an almost unbroken green belt that encompassed Latin America, Africa, Southeast Asia, Indonesia, and Australia and covered about 20 percent of the earth's land surface. Today, rain forests cover less than 7 percent of the earth's land surface, and the once-continuous strip is now broken up into a series of green pockets.

If you look at the map on pages 18 and 19, you can see that these pockets of rain forest lie both north and south of the equator, bordered on the north by the Tropic of Cancer and on the south by the Tropic of Capricorn. Although rain forests grow in more than 50 countries, more than half the total area is found in just three countries: Brazil with 33 percent and Zaire and Indonesia with 10 percent each. (See "Tropical Trivia Trek" on page 10 for more about the location of tropical rain forests.)

WHAT ARE TROPICAL RAIN FORESTS?

Hot, Humid, and Wet: Tropical rain forests are characterized by hot, humid weather throughout the year. By definition, they get more than 80 inches of rain a year, although some areas regularly get more than 200 inches and a few get more than 400! Temperatures sometimes climb into the 90s but usually hover between 70° and 85°F.

In most tropical rain forests, the temperature variation during the year is small, and there is very little variance between daytime highs and nighttime lows. (For more about temperatures in tropical rain forests, see "Forest Comparisons" on page 11.) Consistently high temperatures are characteristic of lands that hug the equator. And unlike other regions of the world, these equatorial areas get more energy from the sun because they experience year-round, 12 hours of daylight, and because the sun's rays strike the equator at right angles, providing more intense and direct sunlight.

Consistently high temperatures and abundant rainfall contribute to another tropical rain forest characteristic—high humidity. In the rain forests of South America, scientists estimate that as much as 250 billion tons of water vapor can be suspended in the air at any one time. The abundant water vapor in tropical rain forests is also a result of a high rate of plant transpiration. On the average, the humidity in a rain forest is about 70 percent during the day and 95 percent at night.

Luxuriant and Diverse: The moist, hot conditions in tropical rain forests support an abundant diversity of plant life—from luxuriant shrubs and ferns to climbing vines and giant trees. The plants, in turn, support an amazingly varied community of wildlife.

Although tropical rain forests cover less than 7 percent of the earth's land surface, scientists estimate that they may house more than 50 percent of all species. In fact, some scientists calculate that this figure could actually be much higher, given the number of new species that are constantly being discovered in tropical rain forests. (For more about tropical rain forest diversity, see the background information on pages 21–23.)

Shallow, Damp, and Infertile: Rain forest soils support an incredible variety of plants, but the soil itself is often not very fertile. Most of the nutrients that are used by plants are stored in the plants themselves, not in the soil. In other types of forests, such as temperate forests, the soils are often much more nutrient rich.

The lack of nutrients in tropical rain forest soil is the result of two things: abundant rainfall and age. In all forests, rain washes away, or leaches, important nutrients from

the soil—but leaching can be an especially serious problem in rain forests becau[se?]
there is so much rain and it comes in such intense and frequent bursts. And in ma[ny]
areas where tropical rain forests grow, the soils are relatively old and have be[en]
leached for millions of years, leaving very few mineral nutrients.

The roots of most rain forest trees are concentrated near the surface of the soil.
dead animals and plants decay (which they do rapidly because of the high temp[er]-
atures and humidity), the trees' shallow roots quickly absorb the nutrients *before* th[ey]
are leached away. Billions of microorganisms that live in the soil help break do[wn]
plant and animal debris quickly into usable nutrients—phosphorus, calcium, potas[si]-
um, and nitrogen. This continual and quick recycling of nutrients is what keeps t[he]
rain forest system working so efficiently.

LAYERS OF LIFE

The trees, shrubs, vines, ferns, and other plants that grow in rain forests form[a]
complex system of layers. Although the layering system varies from area to area a[nd]
the boundaries between layers are often not distinct, a generalized cross section wou[ld]
look something like the diagram in the margin. Here's more about each layer, starti[ng]
at the top and working down.

The Emergents—Giants of the Jungle: Towering above all the other plants in t[he]
forest are the giant trees called *emergents.* Although most emergents are about 115[to]
150 feet tall, some grow to heights of over 250 feet. There are usually only one or tw[o]
of these jungle giants per acre, and characteristically they have relatively small leav[es,]
umbrella-shaped crowns, and tall, slender trunks. Emergents stick out from the cro[wd]
and must endure high and often changing temperatures, low humidity, and stro[ng]
winds.

Many of these jungle giants have unique structures. Some species have thi[ck,]
ridged *buttresses.* Others have long, round *stilt roots* that surround the base of t[he]
trunk. Although no one is sure what purpose the buttresses and stilt roots serve, sor[ne]
scientists think they might help support trees with shallow root systems. (See page [?]
for an illustration of buttresses and stilt roots.)

The Canopy—Treetops of Life: Like a thick green carpet, the main *canopy* layer[of]
the rain forest is formed by flat-crowned trees that are often between 65 and 100 f[eet]
above the ground. Like the emergents, trees in the canopy are subjected to changi[ng]
temperature and humidity. The canopy trees, along with the emergents, form a co[n]-
tinuous covering over the forest. And like emergents, many canopy trees are su[p]-
ported by buttresses and stilt roots.

The canopy acts like a giant sun and rain umbrella. It catches most of the sun's ra[ys,]
allowing only about 2 to 5 percent to slip through to the forest floor. The canopy a[lso]
absorbs much of the impact of the rain that falls on the forest. But the rain doesn't a[c]-
cumulate on the leaves. That's because the leaves of many kinds of canopy trees a[re]
pointed, causing water that hits each leaf to run off. These "drip tips" help keep le[af]
surfaces dry, which discourages the growth of mold, lichens, and small plants.

The canopy is filled with life. The umbrella of leaves and branches provides a ho[me]
for many treetop creatures, as well as for orchids, vines, bromeliads, and a host [of]
other plants. (See "Canopy Critters" on page 24 for more about life in the canop[y.])

The Understory—Life in the Shadows: Below the canopy there are small tre[es]
that usually don't grow to heights of more than 15 feet or so, and a shorter shrub la[yer]
of very young canopy trees and miniature woody plants. Together, these plants ma[ke]
up the *understory.* Some of these understory plants will eventually grow tall enough [to]
become part of the canopy. But others will always remain in the shadow of the cano[py]
giants. Unlike flat-topped canopy trees, many of these understory trees have elo[n]

gated crowns that are shaped like candle flames. Many also have large leaves, which scientists think help the plants absorb as much sunlight as they can in the dim understory.

The Forest Floor—Life at the Bottom: On the *forest floor,* often more than 65 feet below the canopy, the conditions are very different from those at the top. The canopy is subjected to strong sun and plenty of wind, causing considerable daily fluctuations in humidity and temperature. But on the sheltered floor, the air is very still, humidity is almost always above 70 percent, and the temperature remains relatively constant.

Although seedlings, herbs, and ferns grow on the forest floor, the vegetation is fairly sparse—mainly because of lack of sunlight. And although many people think the rain forest floor is littered with decaying logs and thick layers of dead leaves, the floor is actually quite open.

JUNGLE TALK

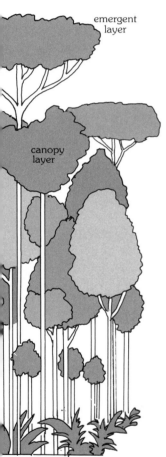

emergent
layer

canopy
layer

forest floor

Getting Tropical Terms Straight: In this issue we will focus on the moist tropical forests that lie close to the equator at low elevations. These forests are commonly called *tropical rain forests.* However, much of what we say about tropical rain forests—especially when we talk about the problems of deforestation—also holds true for two other types of forests found in the tropics: *tropical seasonal forests* and *tropical cloud forests.* Tropical seasonal forests occur throughout the tropics and have two distinct seasons—a wet season and a dry season. They differ from tropical rain forests in that they don't get abundant, year-round rainfall and they experience seasonal periods of drought.

Cloud forests are tropical forests that grow at middle to high elevations. These mountainous jungles are kept moist by mist and clouds, as well as by rain. Found in mountains throughout the tropics, cloud forests are denser and have shorter trees than tropical rain forests, and ferns, mosses, and liverworts often grow more thickly on tree branches. In some areas these forests are better known as "moss forests." Unlike lowland tropical rain forests, cloud forests can become relatively cool.

Jungle Myths: Where does the word "jungle" fit into our tropical rain forest definitions? Etymologists have traced the word to the ancient Sanskrit word "jangala," which was used to describe thick, impenetrable vegetation. Today jungle is the popular term for tropical forests in general. Although many people use the word "jungle" interchangeably with "tropical rain forest," the literal definition of the word misrepresents what a tropical rain forest is actually like. Tropical rain forests are not impenetrable masses of vegetation. Instead, in a mature tropical forest the forest floor is fairly open and uncluttered.

People probably first used the word "jungle" to describe tropical forests when they traveled by boat to explore these areas. Along tropical riverbanks and openings in the forests, tangled "jungle" vegetation does spring up. That's because in open areas, much more sunlight reaches the ground and encourages plant growth. Many early explorers mistakenly assumed that the inside of a rain forest was just like its overgrown edges.

Diverse, Yet Fragile: Tangled undergrowth is not the only rain forest myth that has been perpetuated through the years. Another is that rain forests, with their thick vegetation and abundant wildlife, are "tough" and can withstand changing conditions without serious consequences. Unfortunately, this isn't true, and as more development takes place in the tropics, people are finding out just how fragile rain forest ecosystems are. (See "Lost in the Jungle" on page 14 for more about rain forest myths and "Issues and Answers" on page 58 for more about problems facing tropical rain forests today.)

Figuring Out Forests

Talk about conditions in tropical rain forests; then use symbols to identify some rain forest animals.

Objectives:
Describe several characteristics of tropical rain forests. Name some animals that live in tropical rain forests.

Ages:
Primary

Materials:
- *copies of pages 16 and 17*
- *scissors*
- *paper*
- *pencils*
- *pictures of tropical rain forests*

Subject:
Science

Here's a way to introduce younger kids to tropical rain forests. Before you begin, copy and enlarge each of the general symbols in the margin on page 7 on a separate sheet of paper. These symbols represent rainfall, temperature, and humidity. Then copy each of the symbols at the bottom of page 17 on a separate sheet of paper. These symbols represent conditions in tropical rain forests. (The drawings should be large enough for everyone to see.)

Now use the background information on pages 3–5 to introduce your group to tropical rain forests. Also show the kids pictures of tropical rain forests to give them an idea of what these forests look like.

Next show the kids the enlarged symbols you copied from the margin earlier. (Don't show them the symbols of the rain forest conditions yet—you'll hang those up later.) Explain that these symbols represent certain general conditions in forests. For example, the cloud and raindrops represent the average amount of rain a forest receives in a year. The thermometers show what average daytime temperatures are like in December and in June. Differences between the temperatures on the thermometers represent seasonal temperature differences in the forest. And the steaming kettle represents the average amount of humidity (the amount of moisture in the air) in a forest over the course of a year.

As you explain each symbol to the kid ask them how they could change it t show a forest with different condition For example, ask the kids how they coul adapt the cloud symbol to show a fore that receives more or less rain each yea (draw more or fewer drops) To sho cooler or warmer temperatures, th "mercury" on the thermometers would b lower or higher. And to show a more c less humid forest, there would be more c less steam coming out of the kettle.

Now hang each of the "rain forest con ditions" symbols you copied earlier und its corresponding "general conditions drawing. Explain to the kids that thes symbols show what conditions are like in tropical rain forest. Have the kids compa these symbols to the general symbols an describe the conditions in tropical rain fo ests. For example, the kids should notic that there are lots of raindrops coming o of the cloud and conclude that it rains a l in tropical rain forests. They should notic that the thermometers show high tempe atures and realize that these forests a fairly hot. (Tropical rain forests averag 70°–85°F during the daytime.) Also poi out that both thermometers have near the same temperature, representing th fact that daytime temperatures in tropic rain forests don't change much from or time of year to another. And the kic should notice that a lot of steam is comir out of the kettle, representing the fact th tropical rain forests tend to be very humic

Next pass out pencils, scissors, and copy of pages 16 and 17 to each perso Explain that page 16 (Sheet 1) shows fo different forests from around the worl along with some of the animals that live each one. Page 17 (Sheet 2) shows ju the animals that live in these forests a the tropical rain forest symbols the ki just discussed. Tell the kids that they mu circle the animals on page 17 that live tropical rain forests and put an "X through those that don't. To figure o which animals live in tropical rain fores they must use the symbols of tropical ra forest conditions and page 16. Here how:

orangutan

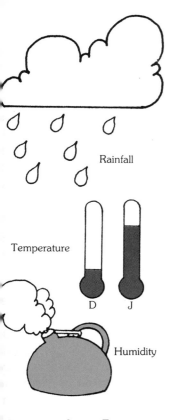

Rainfall

Temperature

D   J

Humidity

First have the kids cut off the strip of symbols on page 17. (Make sure they keep it in one piece.) Then tell them to pick an animal on page 17 and find it in one of the forests on page 16. Next have them compare their strip of tropical rain forest conditions to the strip of conditions underneath the picture of that forest. If all the conditions match, the kids will know that the forest is a tropical rain forest and that the animal does live in tropical rain forests. If the conditions don't match, the forest is not a tropical rain forest. Remind the kids to look carefully at *all* the symbols as they compare them.

After the kids have finished, go over the animals and forests, using the answers on the right. You might want to point out that the animals shown in each scene would not necessarily be seen at the same time of day or in the same place in the forest.

Also, the animals' sizes are not shown in proportion. And you might want to point out to the kids that the general kinds of animals may be found in different kinds of forests, but not the same species. For example, spotted owls are found only in the forests of the Pacific Northwest. But other owls are found in other types of forests around the world.

ANSWERS

A. Southeast Asian Tropical Rain Forest
Asian tapir (TAY-per)—2
flying fox—10
slow loris—12

B. North American Eastern Deciduous Forest
wild turkey—1
southern flying
 squirrel—5
red fox—11

C. North American Pacific Northwest Forest
spotted owl—6
porcupine— 4
clouded salamander—8

D. South American Tropical Rain Forest
agouti (ah-GOO-tee)—3
motmot—7
giant armadillo—9

Jungle Journey

Listen to a story and imagine what it would be like to walk through a tropical rain forest; then draw pictures or create postcards of the trip.

Objectives:

Describe what conditions are like in tropical rain forests. Name some animals that live in these forests.

Ages:

Primary and Intermediate

Materials:

- *story on pages 8 and 9*
- *pictures of tropical rain forests and tropical rain forest plants and animals (see story for suggestions)*
- *drawing paper or large, blank index cards*
- *crayons or markers*

(continued next page)

Y ou might not be able to take your group to a tropical rain forest. But in this activity your kids can take an imaginary trip to one of these forests and discover some of the plants and animals that live there.

Begin by introducing the kids to tropical rain forests. Using the map on pages 18 and 19, explain where these forests grow. Also show the kids pictures of these forests. (You might want to talk about some of the animals that live in a tropical rain forest too.)

Next tell the kids they will be listening to a story about two people who explore a tropical rain forest in Central America. (You might want to point out your location and Central America on a globe.) Tell the kids they must listen carefully to what the people in the story do and see as they explore the jungle.

After you finish reading "A Jungle Journey," discuss what happened in the story. You might want to ask the kids some of the following questions to get them thinking about the story:

- What did the forest look like as Vanessa and her dad were traveling down the river in the boat?
- Once Vanessa and Juanita were inside the forest, what did it look and feel like?
- Describe the moth that Vanessa and Juanita spotted. How might it help the moth to look like this?

Brooke Spencer, 2nd Grade, Spring Hill Elementary School, McLean, Virginia

• *pens or pencils*
• *globe (optional)*

Subjects:
*Science, Language
Arts, and Art*

inchworm moth
leaf-cutter ants
"tank" bromeliad
morpho butterfly
three-toed sloth
common long-tongued bats

• What were the ants in the story doing?
• What did Juanita say made the sloth look green?
• What did Vanessa see inside the hollow tree?
• Vanessa had to stand on tiptoes to look inside one particular plant. What was special about that plant?
• What do you think Vanessa enjoyed most about her walk?

As you discuss the story, show the kids pictures of some of the plants and animals mentioned in it. In the margin, we've listed some of the plants and animals that were referred to in the story.

After the discussion, pass out drawin[g] paper and crayons or markers to the kid[s] and have them draw their favorite part o[f] the story. Afterward have the kids shar[e] their pictures with the group.

If you're working with older kids, hav[e] them make postcards of the trip. First pas[s] out large, blank index cards, crayons o[r] markers, and pens or pencils. Then hav[e] the kids draw something from the story o[n] one side of the index card and write a de[-] scription of something that happene[d] during the trip on the other side. Afte[r]ward have each person "send" his or he[r] postcard to another member of the grou[p].

A JUNGLE JOURNEY

Vanessa clutched the side of the boat as it chugged away from shore. *I'm finally going to see the jungle!* she thought. It seemed so long since her father had said he was going to Central America to study tropical rain forest insects and had told her she could come. And now here they were, riding down a muddy-looking river with jungle on both sides.

As the boat chugged along, Vanessa looked at the plants growing along the riverbank. A solid wall of leaves, trunks, vines, and branches grew on both sides of the river. She had heard that plants grew so thickly in jungles that people had to cut their way through them with big knives. Now she could see why!

It didn't take long for the boat to reach the research station where she and her father would be staying. They collected their gear and went to meet the other people at the station.

The next morning Vanessa's father left very early to collect insects. But he had arranged to have Juanita, another researcher, take Vanessa on a walk in the jungle.

After breakfast, Juanita and

Vanessa set out to explore. Once inside the forest, Vanessa stopped and looked around.

She noticed several things right away—how green the forest was and how dark and still. As she stood there, her eyes adjusted to the dim light. Here and there she could see shafts of sunlight shining to the forest floor, like small spotlights. The rest of the forest was bathed in a kind of greenish-gray light. All around her she could see the dark shapes of tree trunks. The trees were very tall and straight and their lowest branches were high above her head. Higher still, Vanessa could see flecks of light between the leaves of the trees. It seemed as if the leaves formed a roof over the forest.

Looking around her, Vanessa noticed some smaller trees and shrubs. She also noticed ferns and other plants growing on the forest floor. But overall the forest was fairly open and easy to walk through—not at all like the tangle of plants she had seen from the boat the day before. Now she knew what it was *really* like to be in a tropical rain forest.

She'd also noticed that there were plants growing all over the trunks of the trees. Some were almost flat against the tree trunks. Others had leaves like a pineapple top. And others looked like clumps of hair. Huge vines hung between the trees and other vines snaked up the sides of the trees. As Vanessa was looking around, she realized how hot she was. She could feel sweat running down the back of her neck. And there was no wind in the forest to help cool her off.

"Hey, Vanessa! Come here!"
Vanessa stopped looking at the trees and other plants and ran over to where Juanita was standing. She was pointing at some dead leaves on the forest floor.

"Pretty neat, huh?" she asked.
"What?" Vanessa looked at her as if she were crazy. *What does she think is so special about dead leaves?* she wondered.

Then Juanita slid her foot closer and closer to one particular "dead leaf." Suddenly it flew off the ground, fluttered in the air for a minute, and landed on some other dead leaves several yards away.

"Wow!" cried Vanessa as she

went after it, hoping for another look. "That's the best camouflage I've ever seen. What was it?"

"A moth," answered Juanita.

While Vanessa looked for the leaf-shaped moth, she noticed something else on the forest floor. "Hey, Juanita. Look at these ants. What are they doing?"

Juanita came over and looked at the parade of ants. Many of them were carrying little pieces of leaves.

"They're leaf-cutter ants and they're taking the plant pieces to their underground nest. If we follow their trail backwards, we should find the plants they're working on."

It didn't take long for Vanessa and Juanita to find the small tree the ants were working on. Its stems, branches, and leaves were crawling with ants. Vanessa bent over to watch the tiny creatures cut out pieces of leaves and lift them over their heads.

"What do they do with the leaf pieces when they get them back to their nests?" she asked.

"They clean them off and then let fungus grow on them," answered Juanita. And then, because Vanessa looked kind of confused, she added, "The ants *eat* the fungus."

Vanessa had never heard of ants that grew their own food. She stood by the tree and continued to watch them.

"Hey, Vanessa—want to see a living aquarium?" asked Juanita, who had moved over to a larger tree.

"A living *what*?"

Vanessa went over to where Juanita was standing.

"See that plant up there with all the long, pointed leaves?" Juanita asked, pointing to a plant on the tree. "Look inside it."

Vanessa stood on tiptoes and peered into the plant. All the leaves joined together at the base

and formed a kind of cup. The cup was about half full of water. And swimming around in the water were some little creatures Vanessa guessed were insects. There was also a snail crawling around.

"Wow! It *is* like an aquarium."

"This plant is called a bromeliad," said Juanita. "And there are many different kinds. Lizards, snakes, monkeys, and other animals sometimes drink out of them. And frogs even lay their eggs in them!"

Just then a brilliant blue butterfly fluttered slowly by Vanessa and Juanita and landed in a nearby patch of sunlight. After a few seconds the butterfly took off, drifting out of sight.

"That butterfly was so beautiful," Vanessa said. "I never knew anything could be so blue! And . . . hey, what's that clump of stuff up there? I think it just moved."

Juanita looked up in the trees where Vanessa was pointing. "That's a sloth," she said. "They spend almost their whole lives hanging upside down in the trees, eating leaves."

"It looks like a green blob to me."

"Yeah. Sloths have tiny, green algae growing in their fur, which makes the sloths harder to see in all the green leaves. C'mon. There's a hollow tree up here I want you to see."

When Vanessa and Juanita reached the hollow tree, Juanita pulled a flashlight from her belt. She turned it on and carefully

poked her head into a large hole in the side of the tree. Then she pulled her head back out and handed Vanessa the flashlight.

"All clear," she said. "Take a look."

Vanessa took the flashlight and poked her head into the hole. Shining the flashlight upwards, she saw several brown, furry bodies. At first she didn't know what they were. Then a little head turned and looked at her, and she could see they were bats. *Neat-o!* she thought. She slowly turned the flashlight down, lighting up the inner walls of the tree. She saw crickets, giant roaches, and beetles. The "floor" of the tree was covered with dung from the bats, and the dung was covered with more insects, centipedes, and other crawling things.

"Wow!" she cried, pulling her head out of the hole. "There're so many animals living inside this tree. And those bats are so neat!"

"Yeah," said Juanita. "I think they feed on nectar from flowers. Did you know that there are more bats in rain forests than all other mammals *combined*?"

"Wow!" said Vanessa. "I hope I get to see some others before I leave."

"Well, maybe tomorrow. We better start heading back now," said Juanita.

Vanessa sighed. They had explored only a tiny part of the jungle and had seen so much. She could hardly wait to explore more of it tomorrow.

three-toed sloth

Tropical Trivia Trek

Objectives:
Describe where tropical rain forests are located. Name several rain forest animals and plants and tell where they live.

Ages:
Intermediate and Advanced

Materials:
- *copies of pages 18 and 19*
- *atlases and encyclopedias*
- *copies of "Trek Questions" below*
- *pencils*
- *glue*
- *large sheets of construction paper*
- *scissors*
- *large world map*
- *slips of paper*
- *tape*

Subjects:
Science and Geography

B y matching tropical plants and animals to the rain forests where they live, your kids can learn more about where these forests are located. Before starting, make copies of the "Trek Questions" below. Then begin the activity by going over the general characteristics of rain forests with your group, using the background information on pages 3–5. Next give each person a copy of pages 18 and 19. Explain that the shaded areas on the map show where tropical rain forests are located around the world. You may also want to point out the equator, the Tropics of Cancer and Capricorn, and the other lines of latitude.

Tell the kids that the plants and animals pictured around the map live in different tropical rain forests around the world. The information by each picture tells something about that plant or animal. And the location listed under each picture pinpoints one of the countries or areas where the plant or animal is found. (Be sure to explain that most of these plants and animals are found in other places as well. For example, the three-toed sloth is found in other countries besides Ecuador.)

Now provide atlases and encyclopedias. Tell the kids to use these resource materials to find the country or area specified for each plant and animal. Then tell them to match each plant or animal to the rain forest where it lives. As the kids match the pictures, they should write the number of each plant or animal in the correct location on the map. Explain to the kids that if they have no idea where a country is, they should look it up.

After everyone has finished, go over the answers. To do this, use a large world map. First write each number on a separate slip of paper, and then have volunteers take turns attaching each number to the correct spot on the map (see diagram).

Then pass out glue, scissors, and large sheets of construction paper. Tell the kids to cut along the solid lines on pages 18 and 19 so that they have 13 separate pictures and the map. Have them glue their maps in the center of the construction paper, and then have them glue each picture onto the border near the rain forest where each plant or animal lives. To finish up, pass out copies of the "Trek Questions" and have the kids answer them.

TREK QUESTIONS

1. Name several rain forest animals that use special parts of their bodies to help them move around in the forest. (flying frogs have webbed feet that help them glide; sloths have hooklike claws and spider monkeys have grasping tails that help the animals hold on to branches)
2. What are two products that come from tropical rain forests? (chocolate and medicines)
3. Name several continents where tropical rain forests grow. (Asia, Africa, Australia, North America [Central America], South America)
4. Circle the letter of the phrase that *best* describes the location of tropical rain forests. (C)
   A. Most tropical rain forests grow between the latitudes of 30°N and 60°N.
   B. Most tropical rain forests grow between the Tropic of Cancer and the equator.
   C. Most tropical rain forests grow between the Tropic of Cancer and the Tropic of Capricorn.
5. Are there any tropical rain forests in Europe? (no)

Forest Comparisons

Make some observations in a forest in your area; then compare your observations with information about tropical rain forests.

Objectives:
Name several characteristics of a tropical rain forest. Describe two differences and two similarities between a tropical rain forest and a forest in your area.

Ages:
Intermediate and Advanced

Materials:
- *copies of page 20*
- *copies of "Forest Investigations" on page 13*
- *data for weather conditions in your area*
- *wooded area*
- *rain gauge*
- *thermometers*
- *newspaper*
- *paper and pencils*
- *chalkboard or easel paper*
- *world map (optional)*

Subject:
Science

I n this two-part activity, your group can learn what tropical rain forests are like by comparing the conditions in a nearby forest or woodlot with those in a tropical rain forest. (*Note:* Because the kids will need to look at tree leaves, this activity will work best in summer, spring, or fall.)

Before you begin, you'll need data for the average monthly rainfall and temperature of your area. A weather station at a local airport should be able to supply this data. Although you can use monthly averages from a single year, you'll get a look at more typical climate conditions if you use data averaged over several years. You can also request weather information for a specific location from the National Climatic Data Center in Asheville, North Carolina. (There is a small charge for this information.) Call (704) 259-0682 between 8:00 AM and 4:30 PM EST, Monday through Friday. Allow 2–3 weeks for the data to arrive.

PART 1: FOREST FINDS

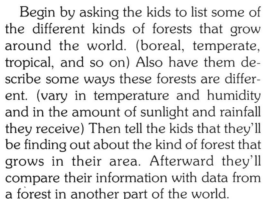

Begin by asking the kids to list some of the different kinds of forests that grow around the world. (boreal, temperate, tropical, and so on) Also have them describe some ways these forests are different. (vary in temperature and humidity and in the amount of sunlight and rainfall they receive) Then tell the kids that they'll be finding out about the kind of forest that grows in their area. Afterward they'll compare their information with data from a forest in another part of the world.

You can have the kids work alone or in small groups. Give each person or group paper, pencils, a thermometer, and a copy of "Forest Investigations" on page 13. Tell them they will be conducting the four investigations in Part 1 now and will use the investigations in Part 2 later. After the kids read over the investigations in Part 1, explain that it will take them several days to gather the data they need. Then take the kids outside to a wooded area and have them get started. Also set up a rain gauge and let the groups take turns checking it each day.

After the kids have finished their observations and have taken weather readings for a few days, write down the kids' results for each of the investigations on a chalk-

Luise Woelflein

board or sheet of easel paper. Also go over how to figure out averages, using the temperature and rainfall data that the kids gathered.

Then pass out copies of page 20 and have the kids graph the monthly average temperature and rainfall data for your area, using the data that you collected from a local weather station. They should use the blank graphs (Graphs A and B) o[n] the Copycat Page.

To finish Part 1, make a list of the gen eral characteristics for forests in your area (For example, a temperate forest is char acterized by temperatures that vary from one season to another; leaves that are o[f] many different shapes; yearly rainfall tha[t] totals about 40 inches; and so on.)

PART 2: LOOKING AT TROPICAL RAIN FORESTS

Explain that the information on the Copycat Page that you passed out earlier was collected by scientists studying a tropical rain forest in Borneo. (You may want to point out where Borneo is on a world map.) Make sure that each person has a copy of the six investigations under Part 2 of "Forest Investigations." Then have the kids answer the questions, using the data they collected, the graphs for temperature and rainfall in your area, and the informa-

tion from the tropical rain forest in Bor neo. After everyone has finished, go ove[r] the answers, using the information unde[r] "Tropical Comparisons." (We've sup plied information about temperate forest[s] in this section. If you live near a boreal o[r] subtropical forest, use information fo[r] your area.) To finish the activity, compar[e] and contrast the characteristics of a tropi cal rain forest with the characteristics o[f] forests in your area.

TROPICAL COMPARISONS

1. You're likely to find a great variety of leaf shapes in many temperate forests, from mitten-shaped sassafras leaves to the needlelike leaves of conifers. But in a tropical rain forest, many leaves have the shape shown on the Copycat Page. Scientists think that pointy tips, called "drip tips," cause water to drain quickly from the leaves, helping to prevent mold, lichens, and small plants from growing on the leaves.

    You might also want to mention that most trees in tropical rain forests are evergreen, whereas many temperate forest trees are deciduous and drop their leaves in the fall. Also, the size of both tropical and temperate forest leaves can vary, depending on where they are found in the forest. Leaves growing in the dim understory tend to be large, which helps them absorb as much sunlight as possible, while many leaves in the sunny canopy are smaller.

2. Answers to these questions will vary, depending on where you live. In general, average temperatures in a temperate area range from about 25°F in the winter to 77°F in the summer.

3. Lowest temperature: 79°F. Highest temperature: 82°F. Temperature difference: 3°F. The temperature varies more in temperate regions. In most tropical

rain forests, temperatures stay between 70° and 85°F throughout the year. (*Note:* These tropical rain forest temperatures were taken on the forest floor, where temperatures change very little. But in the upper canopy and emergent layers of the forest, temperatures may change drastically from day to night and as the weather changes.)

4. Answers will vary, depending on your location. In most temperate regions, an average of about 40 inches of rain falls in a year. The rain forest area in Borneo received 154 inches of rain in a year. By definition, a tropical rain forest receives a minimum of 80 inches of rain each year. And some tropical rain forests get as much as 400 inches of rain in a year!

5. Jan. 1—12 hours, 11 minutes; Mar. 1—12 hours, 3 minutes; May 1—11 hours, 53 minutes; July 1—11 hours, 44 minutes; Sep. 1—12 hours, 1 minute; Nov. 1—12 hours, 10 minutes. (*Note:* The times for sunrise and sunset in Borneo are approximate.)

    In temperate areas, the length of daylight changes throughout the year. But in areas near the equator, where tropical rain forests grow, daylight lasts 12 hours throughout the year.

6. The leaves of many kinds of trees have the same shape; a great deal of rain falls each year; temperatures remain fairly constant throughout the year; daylight lasts about 12 hours all year.

FOREST INVESTIGATIONS

PART 1

1. **Looking at Leaves:** Find as many different kinds of tree leaves as you can and draw their shapes on a piece of paper. You can also collect different kinds of leaves that have fallen to the ground.

2. **What's the Rainfall?** Using a rain gauge, measure the rainfall in your area. At the same time each day, check how much water is in the rain gauge, record this amount, and then empty the rain gauge.

3. **Take the Temperature:** In the same place and at the same time each day, measure and record the temperature.

4. **Day and Night:** Check today's newspaper to find out what time the sun rose this morning and what time it will set this evening. Using these two times, figure out how long daylight will last. Do you think daylight will be the same, longer, or shorter three months from now? Nine months from now?

PART 2

1. Compare the leaves from your area with the leaves from different trees in a tropical rain forest (see Figure 1). What are some differences between the leaves from trees in your area and the leaves from trees in a tropical rain forest? What are some similarities?

2. Look at the graph of the average temperatures in your area (Graph A). What was the lowest temperature and in what month did it occur? What was the highest temperature and in what month did it occur? Subtract the lowest temperature from the highest temperature to find the difference between these two temperatures.

3. Look at the graph showing the average temperatures in a tropical rain forest (Graph C). What was the lowest temperature? What was the highest temperature? Figure out the difference between these two temperatures. Where does the temperature vary more—in your area or in a tropical rain forest?

4. Look at the graph showing average rainfall in your area (Graph B) and add all the months' rainfall together to find the total rainfall in a year. Then look at the graph showing average rainfall in a tropical rain forest (Graph D) and find the total rainfall in a year for this forest. Which had more rain in a year—your area or the tropical rain forest?

5. Look at Figure 2. Using the times for sunrise and sunset, figure out the length of daylight for the first day of each month included on the chart. Write the figure in the blank box under each month. How much does daylight vary in a tropical rain forest compared to day length in your area?

6. Using the data on the Copycat Page and the comparisons you just made, list at least three characteristics of a tropical rain forest.

Lost in the Jungle

Read a short story about a tropical rain forest in Africa and find out what parts of it are accurate and inaccurate.

___

Objective:
Describe some misconceptions about tropical rain forests.

Ages:
Advanced

Materials:
- *copies of page 15*
- *chalkboard or easel paper*
- *reference books*
- *paper and pencils*

Subjects:
Science and Language Arts

Ask most people to describe a jungle and they'll probably mention poisonous snakes, thick undergrowth, and cannibals. Although there is often some truth to jungle stereotypes such as these, many are myths or misconceptions that have been reinforced by popular films and books. In this activity, your kids will read a story that includes many jungle stereotypes, and then do some research to find out what is and isn't accurate about tropical rain forests.

Begin by asking the kids to describe what they think of when they hear the word "jungle," and list their answers on a chalkboard or sheet of easel paper. Next explain that the word "jungle" is used by many people to refer to tropical rain forests. Use the background information on page 3 and the map on pages 18 and 19 to show the kids where tropical rain forests are located, but don't give them any other information yet.

Divide the group into teams of three or four and give each person a copy of page 15. Tell the kids that the story is set in a tropical rain forest. Some parts of the story are accurate, but others are not. Explain that the kids in each team will be working together to find out which parts of the story are accurate and which are inaccurate.

To help the kids get started, go over the first few sentences of the story. For example, point out that they'll first need to find out if it's correct to describe the jungle climate as "hot" and "steamy." They'll also have to check if tropical rain forests grow in Africa and if you would find tigers living in them.

Tell the kids that they should underline all the parts of the story that are inaccurate. And when they've finished checking everything in the story, they should make a list of all the story ideas that were inaccurate and why they were wrong. (*Note:* As they do their research, the kids may be confused by the terms "jungle" and "tropical rain forest." The more accurate term is tropical rain forest. However, many sources use the two terms interchangeably. And a few sources will distinguish between tropical rain forests and jungles. If this happens, the kids should use the information that applies to tropical rain forests.)

After everyone has finished, have each team present their research results for one of the paragraphs or for several sentences. You can use the information in the box titled "The Truth about Tropical Rain Forests" to discuss the accurate and inaccurate parts of each paragraph. Then have the kids use what they've learned to write a story about what they think they'd really see on a journey through the African rain forest.

THE TRUTH ABOUT TROPICAL RAIN FORESTS

Paragraph 1: It's accurate to describe an African rain forest as hot and steamy. (See "Hot, Humid, and Wet" on page 3 for more about the climate in tropical rain forests.) But tigers are found only in Asia.

The description of the forest floor as being dim is accurate. The dense canopy blocks most of the sun's rays, and only a little sunlight reaches the forest floor.

Paragraph 2: Army ants live in Africa and in Central and South America. The African species is commonly called the driver ant. These ants eat mostly caterpillars, grasshoppers, and other small animals. Although they can give a person a nasty bite, army ants don't eat people.

Paragraph 3: In most areas, the rain forest floor is relatively clear. Since very little sunlight reaches the forest floor, few plants grow there. The thick, impassable growth shown in many movies occurs only in open areas with lots of sunlight, such as along riverbanks and in clearings.

It's very unlikely that you would find dozens of different kinds of poisonous snakes in the same place in a tropical rain forest. You also wouldn't find thick layers of dead vegetation on the floor of a tropical rain forest. Dead plant matter is quickly broken down by insects, fungi, and other decomposers.

Paragraph 4: Oranges don't grow wild in the African rain forest. They are native to Asia.

Lions do live in Africa, but only on grassy plains and in dry woodlands—not tropical rain forests. And you wouldn't get far in a tropical rain forest by swinging from vine to vine. Most climbing vines are firmly rooted in the ground and don't hang loosely enough for a person to swing on them.

Paragraph 5: It's true that people known as pygmies live in some African rain forests. But pygmies, like most forest people, don't eat other people. They hunt animals and gather roots, seeds, and berries. (For more about pygmies, see "Forest People" on page 37.)

The hot, steamy air of the African jungle echoed with the growls of a prowling tiger. Although it was the middle of the day, the jungle floor was shadowy and dim. Leafy treetops blocked much of the sunlight.

Two explorers slowly made their way through the jungle. They were lost. Their native guide had been eaten alive by army ants a day earlier. Now, deep in the jungle, the explorers searched for a way out. They hoped to find a river or stream that would lead them back to camp—but none was near.

The explorers' desperate journey was slowed by the thick wall of jungle plants. Swinging sharp machetes, they slashed, inch by inch, through the tangle of vines and tree branches. The sound of slicing machetes startled dozens of different kinds of poisonous snakes that had been resting in the plants. The snakes slithered away through the thick layer of rotting leaves, vines, and branches on the jungle floor.

Exhausted and thirsty, the explorers stopped to cut a few oranges from a nearby tree. As they rested and ate, a great roar suddenly ripped through the steamy jungle. *Lion!* Panicking, the terrified explorers tried to escape by climbing up thick vines and swinging through the air. Like Tarzan, they swung from vine to vine until they were far away. In the distance, they saw the lion slowly disappear through the undergrowth.

Finally, the explorers dropped to the ground. But they weren't out of trouble yet. Still shaking with fright, they didn't hear the approaching steps of the dreaded pygmies. Before they knew it, the explorers were prisoners of the most ruthless cannibals in the jungle.

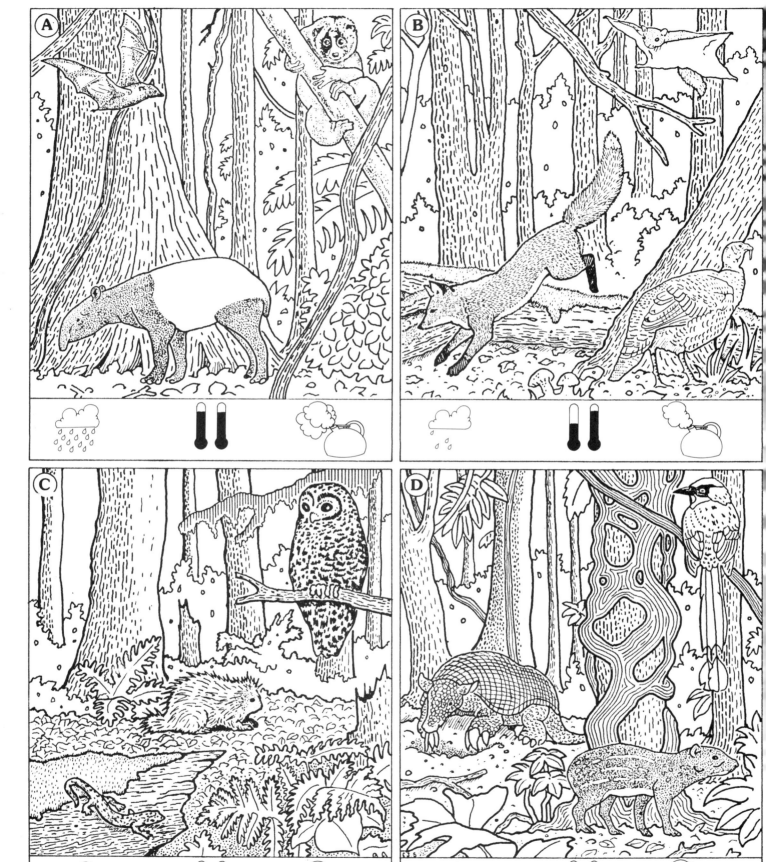

COPYCAT PAGE

1

2

3

4

5

6

7

8
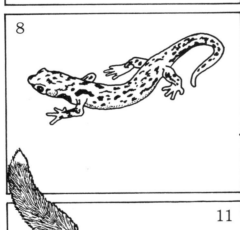

9

10

11

12

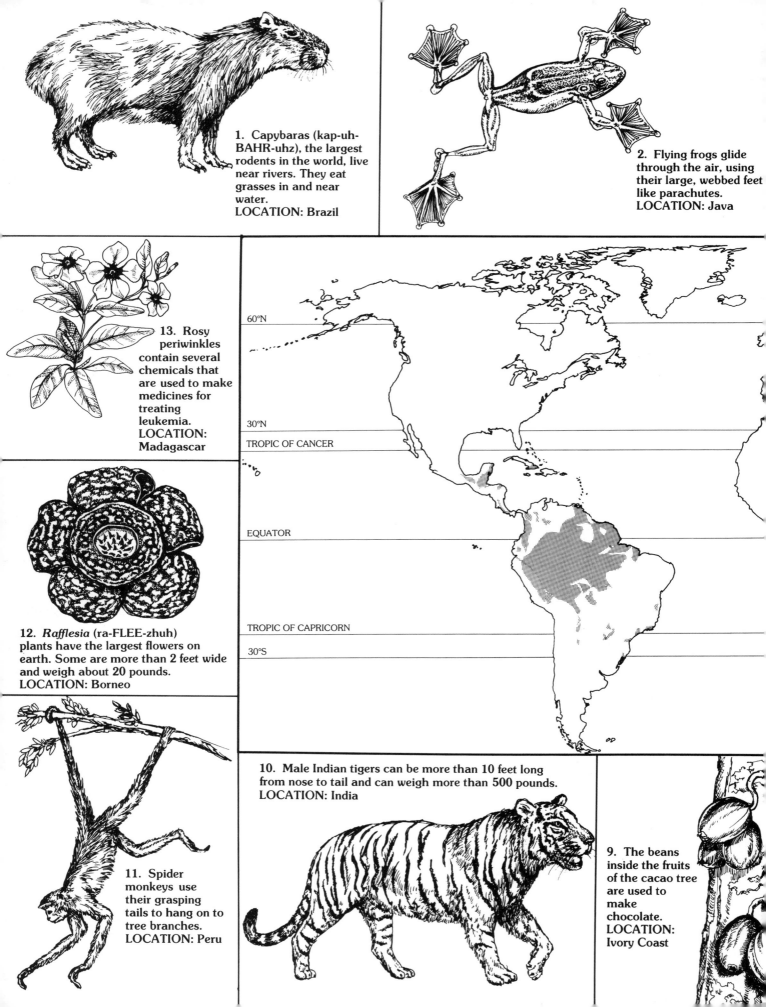

1. Capybaras (kap-uh-BAHR-uhz), the largest rodents in the world, live near rivers. They eat grasses in and near water.
LOCATION: Brazil

2. Flying frogs glide through the air, using their large, webbed feet like parachutes.
LOCATION: Java

13. Rosy periwinkles contain several chemicals that are used to make medicines for treating leukemia.
LOCATION: Madagascar

12. *Rafflesia* (ra-FLEE-zhuh) plants have the largest flowers on earth. Some are more than 2 feet wide and weigh about 20 pounds.
LOCATION: Borneo

11. Spider monkeys use their grasping tails to hang on to tree branches.
LOCATION: Peru

10. Male Indian tigers can be more than 10 feet long from nose to tail and can weigh more than 500 pounds.
LOCATION: India

9. The beans inside the fruits of the cacao tree are used to make chocolate.
LOCATION: Ivory Coast

60°N

30°N

TROPIC OF CANCER

EQUATOR

TROPIC OF CAPRICORN

30°S

Guatemala's national symbol is the resplendent
[quet]zal, a brilliant green and red bird. The males
[hav]e 3-foot-long tail feathers.
[LO]CATION: Guatemala

4. Three-toed sloths eat
only leaves. Their curved,
hooklike claws help them
hold on to tree branches.
LOCATION: Ecuador

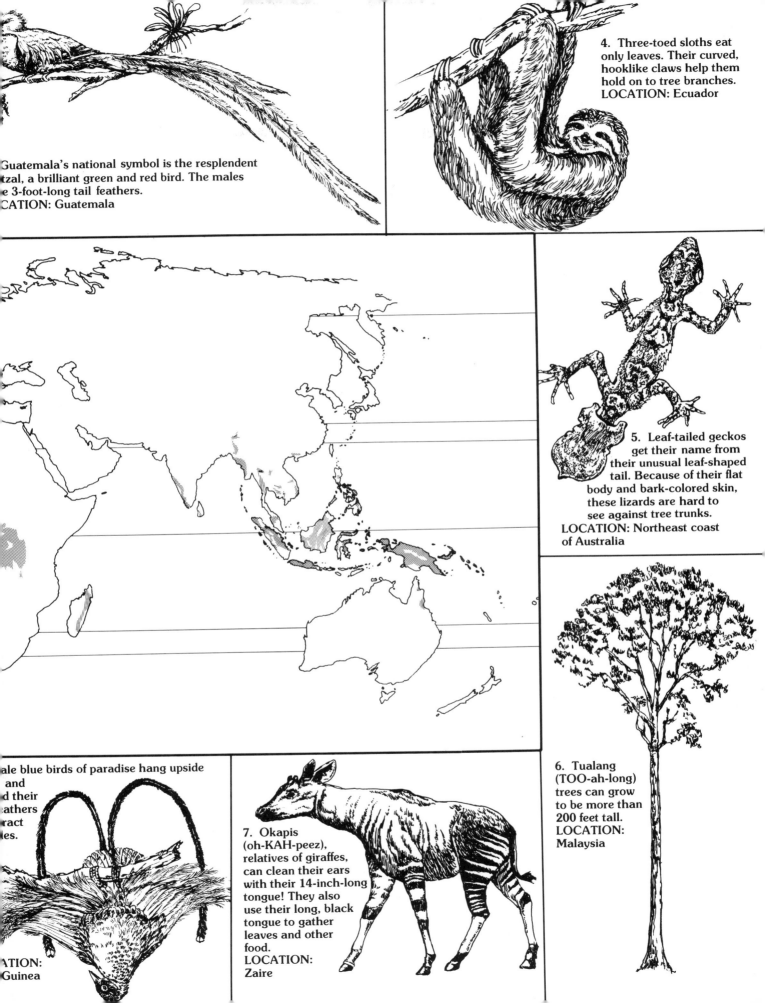

5. Leaf-tailed geckos
get their name from
their unusual leaf-shaped
tail. Because of their flat
body and bark-colored skin,
these lizards are hard to
see against tree trunks.
LOCATION: Northeast coast
of Australia

6. Tualang
(TOO-ah-long)
trees can grow
to be more than
200 feet tall.
LOCATION:
Malaysia

[M]ale blue birds of paradise hang upside
[down] and
[sprea]d their
[fe]athers
[to attr]act
[ma]les.

[LOC]ATION:
[New] Guinea

7. Okapis
(oh-KAH-peez),
relatives of giraffes,
can clean their ears
with their 14-inch-long
tongue! They also
use their long, black
tongue to gather
leaves and other
food.
LOCATION:
Zaire

FOREST COMPARISONS

FIGURE 1

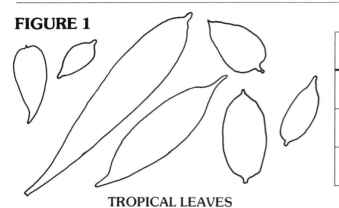

TROPICAL LEAVES

DAY LENGTH IN A TROPICAL RAIN FOREST

MONTH/ DAY	JAN 1	MAR 1	MAY 1	JUL 1	SEP 1	NOV 1
SUNRISE *(AM)*	5:58	6:11	6:01	6:09	6:02	5:41
SUNSET *(PM)*	6:09	6:14	5:54	5:53	6:03	5:51
DAY LENGTH						

FIGURE 2

Graph A AVERAGE TEMPERATURE IN YOUR AREA

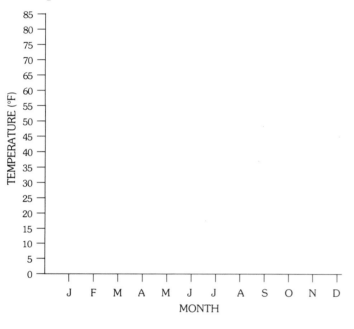

Graph B AVERAGE RAINFALL IN YOUR AREA

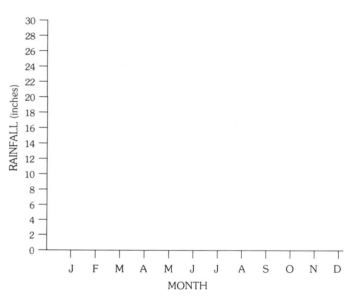

Graph C AVERAGE TEMPERATURE IN A TROPICAL RAIN FOREST

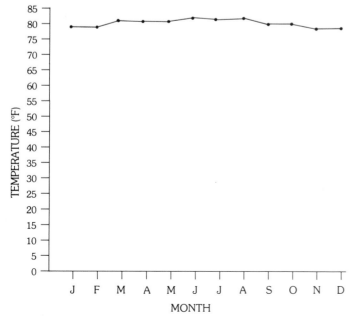

Graph D AVERAGE RAINFALL IN A TROPICAL RAIN FOREST

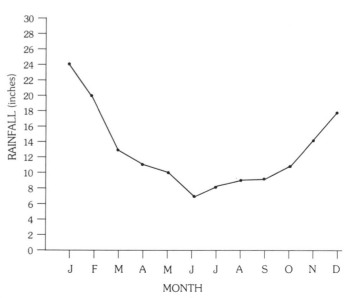

RANGER RICK'S NATURESCOPE: RAIN FORESTS—TROPICAL TREASURES (*See Forest Comparisons*—p 10)

LIFE IN TROPICAL RAIN FORESTS

-tailed macaque

From the sun-kissed leaves of the canopy down to the moss-covered roots of the forest floor, tropical rain forests are loaded with life. Compared to other habitats around the world, rain forests support an incredible number of species: In Ecuador, 20,000 different kinds of plants grow—more species than are found in all of Europe, an area more than 30 times larger. Malaysia, a country in Southeast Asia, boasts 2500 species of trees—three times more than grow in the entire United States. And Peru, a country smaller than Alaska, has more species of mammals than the United States and Canada combined.

With well over half the world's species of animals and plants clustered in less than 7 percent of the world's land area, it's not surprising that rain forest inhabitants have developed some unique strategies for staying alive. In this chapter, we'll take a look at the complex community of life in tropical rain forests.

WHAT MAKES RAIN FORESTS SPECIAL?

Why are tropical rain forests so rich in life? Scientists think it's probably due to the age of these forests (tropical rain forests have existed for tens of millions of years), coupled with ongoing climatic changes. During wet, warm periods of the earth's history, the range of tropical rain forests expanded. But during drier, colder spells, rain forests shrank, forming small, isolated pockets. Many plants and animals in these rain forest pockets gradually evolved into new species. And over millions of years, this cycle of expansion and reduction resulted in a rich diversity of species.

Warmth, Water, and Light: The rain forest's constant warmth, sunlight, and humidity also contribute to the diversity of life. These lush conditions make it possible for a variety of plant species to thrive. This abundant growth, in turn, creates a variety of niches where many animals and other plants can live.

Varied But Rare: Although a great number of species live in rain forests, the majority of them are relatively rare. Even in a large area of rain forest, you'll find few animals or plants of the same species—although you'll probably come across many different *kinds* of animals and plants. Scientists think this natural scarcity is due to the high number of species that live in tropical rain forests, and to the high degree of specialization they've achieved. For example, many plants can grow only in a certain part of the forest where they can get the sunlight and nutrients they need. And most animals live in a specific part of the forest where they feed on only a few kinds of food. So, in a given area of rain forest, only a few individuals of any species can find enough resources to fulfill their needs.

SURVIVAL STRATEGIES

From vines that strangle trees to get the sunlight they need to caterpillars that feed on algae growing in the fur of sloths, rain forest species have evolved some pretty amazing ways of staying alive. In this section, we'll look at some of their specialized survival strategies.

THE PLANTS

As we mentioned in chapter 1, rain forest vegetation grows in layers—with giant emergents and canopy trees towering over shorter understory trees, shrubs, and seedlings. (See "Layers of Life" on page 4 for more about rain forest layers.) The plants that live in each layer have adapted to rain forest conditions by developing variety of "staying alive" techniques.

Growing with Scarce Sunlight: For many tropical rain forest plants, finding place in the sun isn't easy. Some understory plants, including many shrubs, herbs and small trees, are adapted to growing in shade. But many other plants can't mak it in the shade and have developed special strategies for "catching the rays" they nee to survive.

- **The Freeloaders:** Some plants never touch the ground. Instead, they grow o other plants. By being up off the dim forest floor, "closer" to the sun, thes epiphytes can get the sunlight they need. Many ferns, mosses, orchids, bromeliads and even small trees are epiphytes.

- **The Climbers:** Unlike epiphytes, climbing vines are rooted in the ground. Som climbing vines sprout on the forest floor and grow toward patches of sunlight. Othe vines creep straight up a tree toward the sunny canopy, sometimes aided by speci hooks or tendrils that grip the tree's bark. And still others germinate in the canop and grow down to the forest floor.

- **Gap Growers:** Many trees are adapted to waiting. They sprout in the shade o the understory and grow slowly for many years. When a tall canopy tree dies, on or more of these trees-in-waiting will quickly grow to take its place.

  Other kinds of trees, called *pioneers,* specialize in growing in large, sunny gap caused by the fall of one or more trees. Seeds of pioneer species, which may hav been lying dormant in the soil for as long as 10 years, suddenly sprout and grov These fast-growing pioneers quickly shoot up to fill the gap.

High and Dry: Finding enough sunlight isn't the only condition plants must adap to. For example, epiphytes, which aren't rooted in the ground and can't soak up sc moisture, have developed several features that help them get the water they need t survive. Some are able to store water inside their stems. And others have aerial root that absorb moisture right from the air. (For more about plant adaptations, se "Design a Plant" on page 28.)

Leaf Me Alone: Like other plants around the world, rain forest plants hav developed a wide arsenal of weapons to get rid of pests. Some plants produc distasteful and even poisonous chemicals in their leaves that discourage plant-eatin animals. Other plants have sharp spines and prickles that help keep animals away And the slippery bark of some trees makes it tough for strangling vines to get a hold

THE ANIMALS

Finding a place to live. Getting enough to eat. Attracting a mate. Avoidin enemies. As in all habitats, the animals in tropical rain forests are faced with constar challenges. Here's a look at some of the specialized strategies that keep rain fores animals "in business":

A Layered Look at Life: Many rain forest creatures carve out a niche by livin in one particular layer of the rain forest. Toucans and hornbills, for example, nest an feed in the tallest trees of the forest, while peccaries, deer, and other animals spen their entire life on the forest floor. Other forest creatures use a multi-layer approac to find the food and shelter they need. Raccoonlike coatis, for example, will roam a the way from the forest floor to canopy branches in search of a meal.

Dinner Time: Many species reduce competition by feeding on a specific type o food, by feeding in a specific place, or by feeding only during certain times. Fc example, several species of antwrens live in South American forests. They all pre on insects, but each species feeds in a different level of the forest. And in West Africa colobus monkeys and small bearlike pottos feed on fruits and other foods in th treetops—but pottos feed only at night, while colobus monkeys forage during the da

Now You See 'Em . . . : Staying out of sight is another survival strategy—one that's shared by creatures everywhere. But rain forest species exhibit some particularly striking examples of camouflage. For example, one type of preying mantis looks exactly like the petals of an orchid. These bright pink insects hide in the flowers, waiting to pounce on their prey. And some caterpillars look just like bird droppings—a great disguise if you want to fool hungry predators.

A Forest Cacophony: In the rain forest, communication between members of the same species can be tough. Animal populations are usually low, and considerable distances often separate individuals. And the dense leaves of the canopy and dim light of the understory make it even harder for animals to see each other. So instead of using sight, most animals use sound to communicate. The rain forest resounds with the calls of birds, insects, monkeys, and frogs as animals try to attract a mate or warn off intruders.

PLANT AND ANIMAL PARTNERSHIPS

Some of the most amazing rain forest adaptations involve plant and animal partnerships. Scientists are just beginning to unravel the mysteries of these intricate interactions that, for many organisms, mean the difference between life and death.

Pollination Pals: One of the best illustrations of plant and animal partnerships is pollination. From figs to orchids, the majority of rain forest plants depend on animals for pollination. Of course, animal-aided pollination isn't unique to the tropics. But in other habitats, wind does much more of the pollinating. In tropical rain forests, wind pollination is a risky business. Rain forest species are so widely scattered that the chances of pollen successfully reaching a plant of the same species is pretty slim. Besides, there's not much wind beneath the rain forest canopy.

Insects, bats, and birds are the most common pollinators of rain forest plants. And many rain forest plants have developed exclusive pollination partnerships. For example, each of the more than 900 species of fig trees around the world is pollinated by a different species of fig wasp.

Sowing Seeds: Plants and animals have also formed seed-sowing partnerships. Although a few rain forest plants, such as tall canopy trees and high-growing epiphytes, produce small seeds that are dispersed by wind, most rain forest plants rely on animals to disperse their seeds. These seeds are often encased in fruits that attract a specific kind of animal. Birds are usually attracted to brightly colored fruits, while bats and some other animals are drawn to fruits with strong odors. The fleshy outer fruits are digested and the seed is regurgitated or later passed unharmed through the animal's digestive system.

One-Upmanship: Plants are constantly evolving adaptations to help deter animal pests. And animals are constantly evolving new strategies that overcome new plant defenses. For example, some species of caterpillars will, after many generations, become immune to the poisonous leaves of certain vines. And some monkeys can safely digest many types of poisonous leaves and fruits.

A FRAGILE COMPLEXITY

Intricate relationships between plants and animals help a variety of species reproduce, find food, and defend themselves. But they also make tropical rain forests very fragile. In many cases, the removal of just one species can disrupt the lives of many other species. This makes preservation of tropical rain forests particularly complex. Scientists are discovering that many rain forest species can be saved only by setting aside large chunks of forest. See "Sizing Up Reserves" on page 28 of *NatureScope—Endangered Species: Wild and Rare* for a look at how life in a rain forest changes when part of the forest is cut down. Also see chapter 4 for information about some of the ways people are working to protect tropical rain forests.

Canopy Critters

Identify some African rain forest animals by listening to descriptive poems.

Objective:
Describe several tropical rain forest animals.

Ages:
Primary

Materials:
- *copies of page 33*
- *pencils*
- *globe (optional)*
- *materials for making a canopy*

Subject:
Science

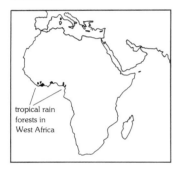
tropical rain forests in West Africa

The treetops of tropical rain forests are crawling with thousands of different creatures. In this activity the kids in your group can find out about some of these animals as they listen to a series of "canopy critter" poems. (Before you get started, you may want to do "Figuring Out Forests" on page 6 with the kids to introduce them to tropical rain forests.)

Begin by passing out a copy of page 33 to each child. Explain that the scene shows some animals that live in the treetops of tropical rain forests in West Africa. (You might want to point out your location and West Africa on a globe.) Then tell the kids that you'll be reading a short poem about each of the animals. The kids must listen carefully to each poem to figure out which animal is being described.

When you finish reading the first poem, have the kids write "1" in the blank near the animal that they think was being described. Before going on to the rest of the poems, you may want to go over the first one to discuss what clues helped the kids make their decision. Then read each of the other poems and have the kids put numbers in the appropriate blanks.

After you've read all the poems, ask the kids some comparison questions to reinforce what they heard in the poems. For example, you could ask the kids to name two animals that have sharp claws, or two animals that fly. (For more about how animals get around in the treetops, see "Treetop Traffic" on page 36 in *NatureScope—Trees Are Terrific!*)

BRANCHING OUT: CANOPY CREATION

Now that your kids know more about some of the creatures that live in the treetops in African rain forests, let them build their own canopy in a corner of your room. Tape green streamers across the room to represent the branches and intertwined vines of the canopy. Then have the kids cut out animal shapes from butcher paper. They can tape or tie their creatures to the "canopy."

CRITTER POEMS

1—E. Dwarf Bush Baby
My great big round eyes
Help me see in dim light
As I search for my prey
In the dark of the night.
My big ears can hear
The softest of sounds.
And I move through the trees
In great leaping bounds.

2—D. Long-Tailed Pangolin
My long, scaly tail
Helps me grab hold of trees
As I move here and there,
Wherever I please.
My super-sharp claws
Can open the nests
Of termites and ants—
The foods I like best.

3—A. Gold's Tree Cobra
My shiny, black body
Can be 7 feet long.
And my fangs inject prey
With a poison that's strong.
I slither through treetops
At night when it's dark.
And the scales on my body
Help me grip the trees' bark.

4—F. African Gray Parrot
Tree seeds and fruits
Are my favorites to eat.
I hold on to these foods
With my scaly, clawed feet.
I climb through the treetops
And nibble all day
Then I finally fly back
To my roost far away.

5—C. Scaly-Tailed Flying Squirrel
The scales on my tail
And a claw on each toe
Help me grip limbs and tree bark
Wherever I go.
Loose skin on my sides
Helps me glide through the air.
I am active at night
And I'm also quite rare.

6—B. African Giant Swallowtail
Way up in the treetops
I flutter around
But you might also find me
Way down on the ground.
I have 9-inch-wide wings
And my colors are bright
I'm orange and black
With some yellow and white.

The Rain Forest Revue

Perform rain forest songs, chants, and poems.

Objectives:
Discuss several characteristics of rain forests. Name several rain forest animals.

Ages:
Primary and intermediate

Materials:
pictures of tropical rain forests and rain forest plants and animals (see activity for suggestions)
copies of the narration, poems, chants, and songs on pages 26 and 27
art supplies for making props
reference books

Subjects:
Science, Language Arts, Music, and Art

Putting on a variety show is a great way for kids to learn about tropical rain forests and some of the incredible animals that live in them. To get the kids started, assign a different group of kids to one of the performances printed under "The Rain Forest Revue" on the next page. (See the "Performance Tips" below for ideas on how many kids to assign to each group.) Or let the kids choose which performances they would like to do. And if you're working with older kids, you may want to have them try creating their own songs, poems, or chants to add to the show.

Give the kids time to research their topics and to draw pictures and create props and costumes to use during the performance. Then have them put on the "The Rain Forest Revue" for other kids and/or their parents.

PERFORMANCE TIPS

Narrator: You might want to split up the narration among several people, with each person being responsible for saying a different block of narrator copy.

"Jungle Rain" Group: This rhythmic chant works well with two or more kids in charge of saying each verse and performing the corresponding movements.

"World above the Ground" Group: Four to six kids is a good number of performers for this song. You might want to have two or three kids sing the first two verses and two or three sing the last two, and then have all of the kids repeat the first verse. The audience and kids who aren't singing can shout the "echoing" phrases at the end of the first, second, and last lines of each verse.

"Day and Night in the Jungle" Group: Try having three pairs of kids take turns saying two lines of this poem. For example, the first pair could recite the first two lines: "In the daytime, monkeys swing." The next pair could recite "Sloths cling, songbirds sing," and so on until the end of the "daytime verse." Then the first pair could start the "nighttime verse" by reciting the first two lines, followed by the next pair, and so on until the end of the poem.

"The Okapi" and "Blue Bird of Paradise" Groups: Any number of kids can perform these limericks. You might want to suggest that some kids act out the animals while others recite the lines.

"The Leaf-Cutter Ants' Parade" Group: Either a small or large group can perform this song. But before the kids perform, have one or more of them talk about leaf-cutter ants and how the ants use leaves to grow fungus "gardens" for food. (For more about leaf-cutter ants, see scenario 4 under "What's Happening Here?" on page 31.) You may also want to have the kids add marching steps or other movements.

Betty Olivolo

Luise Woelflein

JUNGLE RAIN

Narrator: Ladies and gentlemen, welcome to "The Rain Forest Revue." Today we'll be taking you on a journey into the exciting and mysterious world of tropical rain forests—a world where it's warm and green year-round and where it rains nearly every day.

Drip, drop, pour, and patter
Plip, plop, spit, and spatter
Drizzle, drazzle, drain
Jungle rain

snap fingers in rhythm

Slip, slop, ripple, run
Trickle down, fall upon
Leaf and limb and flower
Jungle shower

rub hands together in rhythm, getting faster

Crash, smash, lightning flash
Raindrops splash, creatures dash
Sticky, steamy, warm
Jungle storm

pat knees in rhythm, getting even faster

Rivers run, full and flowing
Plants are lush, green, and growing
Clouds begin to fizzle
Jungle drizzle

rub hands together in rhythm, getting slower

Sun comes out, shines and gleams
Scattered drops and rising steam
Are all that now remain
Of jungle rain

all groups say— rhythms slow down and finally stop

WORLD ABOVE THE GROUND

Narrator: All the rain and warmth in the rain forest means that trees and other plants are green and growing year-round. Many of the trees become giants, forming a thick layer of leaves, branches, and flowers high above the forest floor. This leafy forest covering, called the *canopy,* is loaded with life!

(Sing to the tune of "When You're Happy and You Know It")

In the jungle there's a world above the
  ground
(Above the ground!—say it out loud)
In the jungle there's a world above the
  ground
(Above the ground!)
Leaves and branches touch the sky
In the canopy so high
In the jungle there's a world above the
  ground.
(Above the ground!)

The canopy is plush and lush and
  green
(Lush and green!)
The canopy is plush and lush and
  green
(Lush and green!)
Nearly 60 feet or more
Up above the jungle floor
The canopy is plush and lush and
  green.
(Lush and green!)

The canopy is home to many beasts
(Many beasts!)
The canopy is home to many beasts
(Many beasts!)
Some may never, ever go
To the forest floor below
The canopy is home to many beasts.
(Many beasts!)

They leap and climb and fly among
  the trees
(Among the trees!)
They leap and climb and fly among
  the trees
(Among the trees!)
Monkeys, spiders, sloths, and slugs
Frogs and snakes and birds and bugs
They leap and climb and fly among
  the trees.
(Among the trees!)

All groups repeat the first verse
together.

Narrator: From the canopy to the forest floor, many different kinds of animals live in tropical rain forests. But not all of these animals are out and about at the same time. For example, some rain forest creatures are active during the day and sleep at night. Other rain forest animals sleep all day long and come out when it gets dark.

DAY AND NIGHT IN THE JUNGLE

In the daytime
Monkeys swing
Sloths cling
Songbirds sing.

Orchids bloom
Insects zoom
Parrots chatter
Raindrops patter.

Snakes slide
Lizards glide
And nighttime creatures
Sleep and hide.

In the nighttime
Big cats growl
Owls holler,
hoot, and howl.

Spiders crawl
Night birds call
Insects click
Crickets "crick."

Bats beep
Frogs leap
And daytime creatures
Hide and sleep.

Narrator: Many scientists feel that some of the world's most interesting and beautiful animals live in rain forests. Did you know that rain forests are home to gorillas, toucans, orangutans, and all kinds of cats, bats, birds, insects, and other animals? Some of these species are so amazing it's hard to believe they're real.

THE OKAPI (oh-KAH-pee)

A strange animal is the okapi
With its stripes and its ears big and
  floppy.
It seems that whoever
Put it all together
Got tired or maybe just sloppy.

The okapi's a sight, but don't laugh—
It's a relative of the giraffe.
It eats leaves by the dozen
Just like its tall cousin,
But its neck is shorter by half.

BLUE BIRD OF PARADISE

In far away jungles, I've heard,
Lives a strange and mysterious bird.
It hangs from a tree
Upside down, so you see—
Its behavior is truly absurd.

This jungle bird puts on a show;
It shimmies and shakes to and fro.
It jostles and jiggles,
It waggles and wiggles,
Its long, silky plumes seem to glow.

You may wonder just why it should be
That a bird acts so strange—
Well, you see,
It hangs from a tree
Because it's a he
And he wants to impress a she.

THE LEAF-CUTTER ANTS' PARADE

(Sing to the tune of "When Johnny Comes Marching Home")

The ants go marching back and forth
Hooray, hooray!
The ants go marching south and north
Hooray, hooray!
The ants go marching east and west
Looking for leaves to take back to their
  nest
And they all go marching—
The leaf-cutter ants' parade.

The ants go marching day and night
Hooray, hooray!
The ants go marching, what a sight
Hooray, hooray!
They munch and they crunch and they
  bite and they tear
Cutting up leaves that they find here
  and there
And they all go marching—
The leaf-cutter ants' parade.

The gardens are growing underground
Hooray, hooray!
The gardens are growing underground
Hooray, hooray!
The gardens are growing underground
All over the leaves that the leaf cutters
  found
And they all go marching—
The leaf-cutter ants' parade.

(continued next page)

Narrator: Ladies and gentlemen, we hope you've enjoyed our show! And we hope you'll help protect these special habitats so that there will always be rain forests full of marching ants, beautiful birds, incredible okapis, and all kinds of other fascinating creatures. Thanks for coming to our performance!

27

Here are two other tropical rain forest performance ideas for intermediate and advanced groups:

Yanomamo: Named after the largest remaining tribe of indigenous rain forest people in South America, the musical "Yanomamo" focuses on many of the causes and consequences of deforestation. Commissioned by the World Wildlife Fund-UK and published in London by Josef Weinberger, Ltd., "Yanomamo" is a series of songs with accompanying narration. For information on ordering the musical score and cassette tape of "Yanomamo," write to the Customer Service Department of Boosey and Hawkes, Inc., 52 Coope Square, 10th Floor, New York, NY 10003 7102.

The Tamarin Trickster: This play i about the golden lion tamarin, a tiny en dangered monkey that lives in the Atlanti coastal forest of Brazil. Originally per formed by schoolchildren in Brazil, the pla has been translated and adapted for Nort American audiences. You can find ou more about "The Tamarin Trickster" an about tamarin captive breeding efforts b writing to the Office of Education, Nationa Zoo, 3001 Connecticut Ave., NW, Wash ington, DC 20008.

Art by Amanda Wood for WWF-UK.

scene from "The Tamarin Trickster

Design a Plant

Design a plant that might be able to live in a tropical rain forest.

Objective:
Describe several ways plants are adapted to living in tropical rain forests.

Ages:
Intermediate and Advanced

Materials:
- *chalkboard or easel paper*
- *copies of "Conditions in the Forest" on page 30*
- *drawing paper*

What's it like to live in a tropical rain forest? In this activity the kids in your group can take a "plant's-eye" view of rain forest conditions—such as lots of rainfall and varying amounts of humidity and sunlight—and discover how plants are adapted to them.

Before you get started, copy the questions on page 29 onto a chalkboard or sheet of easel paper. Then begin by discussing tropical rain forests with the kids. Using the background information on pages 3–5, explain where these forests grow and what they are like in general. Also discuss the different layers of vegetation that are found in rain forests. (Be sure to explain that in tropical rain forests the layers are sometimes not distinct.)

Next introduce the term "adaptation to the kids. Explain that all living thing have characteristics that help them sur vive. These characteristics are called ad aptations. For example, tigers' claws hel them catch their prey, and owls' larg eyes help them see in the dark. Ask th kids to name some other animal adapta tions. Then talk about plant adaptations For example, Venus flytraps have specia ized leaves that trap insects, and mos cactuses have spines that protect ther from hungry animals.

Now pass out copies of "Conditions i the Forest" at the top of page 30. Explai to the kids that the list includes many of th conditions tropical rain forest plants mu cope with. Give the kids a chance to rea through the list and then discuss an

buttresses

stilt roots

questions they may have. For example, you may want to review photosynthesis with the kids.

Next tell the kids that, taking these factors into consideration, each person should create and draw an imaginary plant that's adapted to living in a tropical rain forest. They can draw a tree, a shrub, or any other kind of plant. But as they create their plants, they should think about where the plant grows (forest floor, understory, canopy, emergent layer) and what kinds of leaves, roots, branches, and so on it has. Also point out the questions you copied earlier and explain that the kids should be able to answer each of these questions about their plants. Have them label their pictures to help explain their plants' adaptations.

When the kids have finished, have them share their plants with the rest of the group. Then use the information under "Real Plants" below to discuss some general adaptations of plants in tropical rain forests.

QUESTIONS

- Where in the forest does your plant grow?
- Does your plant need sunlight to survive? How does it get the sunlight it needs?
- How does your plant get the water it needs to survive?
- How does your plant keep water from collecting on its leaves?
- How does your plant get the nutrients it needs to survive?
- How does your plant defend itself against hungry insects and other animals?
- If your plant is a canopy tree, how does it keep from being blown over by strong winds?

REAL PLANTS

Searching for Sunshine: Emergent and canopy trees are tall, and their leaves are bathed in sunlight. Bromeliads, orchids, ferns, mosses, and many other *epiphytes* grow on the branches and trunks of these giants, giving them easy access to the sun. Lianas and other vines grow on these trees too, often creeping up the trunks from the forest floor or starting out as a seed in the treetops and dropping roots to the ground. Many of these vines string from tree to tree, "tying" trees together. And if one tree in the forest falls it often pulls others down with it.

Plants in the understory are adapted to living with little sunlight. Many of these plants have broad, flat leaves that absorb as much light as possible. And some plants in tropical rain forests don't need sunlight to survive. They absorb food and nutrients directly from other plants.
Getting Nutrients: Some ferns, bromeliads, orchids, and other epiphytes grow in basketlike shapes that

trap falling bits of vegetation, insects, and other litter. These plants can absorb nutrients from the litter they collect. Some rain forest trees sprout roots from their branches. These roots absorb nutrients from the litter that collects around the bases of epiphytes.
Dripping Tips: Many plants in tropical rain forests have elongated leaves that taper to pointed "drip tips." When water falls on these leaves, it runs down and drips off the end, keeping the leaf free of moisture. Many rain forest plants also have smooth, waxy leaves, which may help get rid of excess water.
Woody Support: Many trees in tropical rain forests have large *buttresses* or sticklike *stilt roots* that flare out from their trunks (see diagram above). Some scientists believe these buttresses and stilt roots help keep the tree from being blown over by spreading the weight of the tree over a broad area and providing support.

Dealing with Pests: Like plants in other habitats, many plants in tropical rain forests produce chemicals in their leaves that make them distasteful or poisonous to plant-eating insects and other animals. Some plants also have spines on their leaves or thorns on their stems, which discourage plant-eating animals. And some get protection from ants that live inside them. For example, ants that live in the spines of certain types of plants in Latin America and Africa will attack animals that touch the tree.
Coping without Water: Much of the rain that falls in rain forests eventually soaks into the soil. Epiphytes, which aren't rooted in the ground, can't soak up soil moisture and must be able to survive without water between rains. Some epiphytes, such as certain orchids, are able to store water inside their stems. The leaves of some bromeliads grow together, forming a "container" that fills with water when it rains. And some orchids and other plants have aerial roots that absorb moisture right from the air.

- Green plants use sunlight to make their own food through a process called photosynthesis.

- Many tropical rain forest trees have shallow roots that don't provide much support.

- Only a small amount of sunlight can get through the canopy, so the inside of the forest is often dim. The air is still, warm, and humid.

- Tree branches in the canopy get more sunlight than those in the understory.

- The air is drier and the wind blows much more in the canopy than in the understory. Sometimes the wind blows trees over.

- Tropical rain forests get a lot of rain. If water stays on plant leaves, it may enable mold, lichens, and small plants to grow on the leaves, which can reduce the light the leaves need for photosynthesis.

- Plants need nutrients to grow. They usually absorb nutrients and water through their roots.

- There aren't many nutrients in most tropical rain forest soils. Almost all the nutrients in these forests are "locked up" in living plants and animals. When rain forest plants and animals die, decomposers quickly break them down. The nutrients stored in them are soon absorbed by rain forest plants.

- Trees in the canopy are often 65 feet tall or taller.

- It takes a lot of energy and nutrients for a plant to grow tall enough to reach the canopy.

- Millions of different kinds of insects live in tropical rain forests. Many of these insects, as well as other animals, eat the leaves and other parts of plants.

Jungle Sleuths

Answer questions and formulate hypotheses about tropical rain forest creatures.

Objectives:
Name several rain forest animals and describe how they depend on other species to survive.

Ages:
Advanced

Materials:
- *copies of the scenarios on pages 31 and 32*
- *pictures of tropical rain forests (optional)*

Subject:
Science

Ants that farm fungus. Bees that "wear" perfume. Butterflies that fool predators by looking like other species. Tropical rain forests are full of these and other strange and amazing animals and plants. In this activity the kids in your group will learn more about these unusual creatures and how they interact with other living things.

Begin by discussing tropical rain forests with the kids. You might want to do several of the activities in chapter 1 to teach the kids where these forests grow and what they're like. You might also want to show the kids pictures of some tropical rain forests in different parts of the world.

Now pass out copies of the scenarios on pages 31 and 32 to the kids. Explain that there are four different scenarios about tropical rain forest plants and animals. The kids should read each one and follow the directions that go along with it. For example, in one scenario they might have to answer questions and in another they might have to solve a problem.

When the kids have finished, go over each scenario, using the information under "What's Happening Here?" on the top of the next page.

orchid bee

WHAT'S HAPPENING HERE?

leaf-cutter ant

Scenario 1

1. Since predators tend to avoid ithomiine butterflies, an edible butterfly that looks like an ithomiine would have a good chance of being avoided too.

2. If there are more edible look-alikes than true ithomiine butterflies living in a forest, it's more likely that the ithomiines would be hunted. That's because a predator would be more likely to have caught tasty butterflies than true ithomiines in the past, and would associate the coloration pattern with good taste instead of bad.

3. If a predator tries to eat a bad-tasting ithomiine butterfly look-alike, it will learn that the butterfly's pattern means bad taste. And it will learn to avoid ithomiines at the same time.

Scenario 2

The experiments will depend on the hypotheses the kids come up with. For example, possible experiments to test if scent or displays attract the females might include collecting males and putting them in a sack or other container so that the females can't see the males but can smell them, and collecting males and putting them in clear, airtight cages so that females can see the displays but can't smell the males.

As mentioned in the scenario, scientists are not sure exactly how the females are attracted to the males. Many scientists believe the males use the oily perfumes to make special chemicals called *pheromones* and that the pheromones attract the females. The displays of the territorial males may also help the females find the males once the females get fairly close.

Scenario 3

Durian tree—flying fox; *Angraecum* orchid—hawk moth; *Brownea* tree—hermit hummingbird. For more about pollination in tropical rain forests, see "Pollination Pals" on page 23.

Scenario 4

Leaf-cutter ants grow fungus in their underground nests. They chew up bits of leaves, stems, and flowers, which they cut from certain types of plants. These chewed-up plant parts serve as a kind of compost for the fungus to grow in. Then they eat some of the fungus. The fungus wouldn't be able to use the nutrients in the leaves if the ants didn't chew them first.

SUPER-SLEUTH SCENARIOS

1 The bright colors and bold patterns of ithomiine (ih-THO-mee-ine) butterflies aren't just pretty decorations. They actually warn would-be predators that the butterflies contain poisonous chemicals and taste bad. (If a bird or other predator catches one of these butterflies it will spit the butterfly out. And it will learn that butterflies with this pattern taste bad.)

In the rain forests where ithomiines live, there are other butterflies that look almost exactly the same as the ithomiines. But these "mimics" don't taste bad and aren't poisonous.

1. Why might it benefit an edible butterfly to look like an ithomiine butterfly?
2. Imagine you're an ithomiine butterfly living in a forest full of edible butterflies that look just like you. Also imagine that there are more of these edible butterflies in the forest than there are poisonous ones like you. Is it more likely that you'll be hunted or avoided by predators? Why?
3. In the forests where the ithomiines live, there are other kinds of poisonous butterflies that look like ithomiines. Why might it be advantageous for the *ithomiines* to have these poisonous look-alikes?

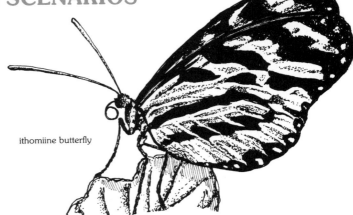

ithomiine butterfly

2 In Central and South American rain forests, brilliantly colored male orchid bees fly from orchid to orchid, collecting oily perfumes from the flowers with pads on their legs. Some of these males stake out a mating territory and fly in unusual patterns and buzz noisily. Females are attracted to these males.

No one knows exactly why or how the females are attracted to the males. It's possible that the females are attracted by the sight and sound of the male displays, by the scent of the males, or in some other way. Come up with a hypothesis to explain how the females are attracted to the males and design an experiment to test your hypothesis.

3 In tropical rain forests around the world, many animals transfer pollen from plant to plant, enabling plants to produce seeds. Many flowers are shaped in certain ways or have particular colors or smells that attract specific animals. For example, some flowers smell like rotting meat, which attracts pollinating flies. Each of the following plants is pollinated by just one of the animals listed. Given the descriptions of the different flowers and animals, match each plant to its pollinator.

PLANT
durian tree
Angraecum (an-GRAY-come) orchid
Brownea (BROWN-ee-ah) tree

POLLINATOR
hawk moth
hermit hummingbird
flying fox (a type of bat)

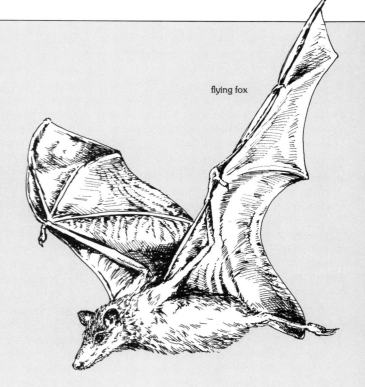

flying fox

- Durian tree flowers and *Angraecum* orchids are white; *Brownea* tree flowers are bright red.

- *Brownea* tree flowers have no scent; *Angraecum* orchids have sweet-smelling flowers; and durian tree flowers are musty smelling.

- The nectar in *Angraecum* orchids is located at the end of a tube that may be 12 inches long.

- Hawk moths and flying foxes are active at night.

- Hermit hummingbirds have long bills.

- Durian tree flowers and *Angraecum* orchids open only at night.

- White flowers are easier to see at night than dark-colored flowers.

- Hawk moths have a long tongue that they can uncoil.

- Bats are usually attracted to musty-smelling flowers.

- Hermit hummingbirds are active only during the day.

4 In a Central American rain forest, leaf-cutter ants visit certain plants. They cut off pieces of leaves, stems, and flowers from the plants and carry the pieces back to their underground nests. There they clean and chew up the plant parts and put them into piles. Given the following information, why do you think these ants bring these plant pieces back to their nests?

- Leaf-cutter ants don't eat leaves, stems, or flowers.

- No one has ever seen these ants eating outside their nests.

- Leaf-cutter ants take leaves, stems, and flowers from only certain kinds of plants.

- Scientists have tested the leaves of some of the plants the ants don't use and have discovered that the leaves have natural fungicides (chemicals that will kill fungus) in them.

- Mounds of fungus grow inside leaf-cutter ant nests.

- If scientists remove the fungus growing in the ant nests, the ants die.

- If scientists remove the ants from their nest, the fungus growing in the nest dies.

(See Canopy Critters—p 24)

PEOPLE & TROPICAL RAIN FORESTS

While exploring the Amazon basin during the mid-1700s, French scie[ntist] Charles Marie de la Condamine saw native people using a stran[ge] sticky substance that they'd extracted from a species of rain forest tr[ee] Fascinated, La Condamine recorded his impressions in his journa[l]

"What renders it most remarkable," he wrote, "is its great elasticity. They [t] Indians] make bottles thereof which it is not easy to break; boots and hollow bo[ots] which may be squeez'd flat, and when no longer under restraint recover their f[irst] form."

La Condamine brought samples of the substance with him back to Euro[pe.] Eventually, scientists found many important uses for this rain forest pro[d]uct—dubbed "rubber" because of its ability to rub out pencil marks.

La Condamine was one of many rain forest explorers. But although explore[rs] adventurers, and scientists have been visiting these special habitats for centur[ies] jungles and their native residents are still just as mysterious in some ways as th[ey] were when the first non-natives stepped within their realms hundreds of years a[go.] And although rain forests have enriched our lives with hundreds of valuable pro[d]ucts (they've given us not only rubber, but also fibers, foods, medicines, and mu[ch] more), most scientists believe these forests harbor a wealth of goods yet to be d[is]covered. That's one of the most exciting things about rain forests: There's still [so] much we can learn and gain from them—and from the people who live in the[m.]

LIVING IN THE RAIN FOREST

One of the great ancient civilizations of the New World—the Maya—flourish[ed] for more than 600 years in the rain forests of southern Mexico and Cent[ral] America. From about A.D. 250 to about A.D. 900, this rich and complex socie[ty] produced a wealth of cultural accomplishments: a 365-day calendar, a written la[n]guage, expertly engineered and ornately carved temples, and the mathemati[cal] concept of zero.

Today, many Mayans still live in Central American rain forests. Oth[er] Amerindians live in the rain forests of South America. And elsewhere in the tropi[cs] other people make a living in jungles: the Mbuti Pygmies of central Africa, the Lu[a'] of Thailand, and the Penan of Borneo, to name a few.

Forest Farmers: One of the most prevalent ways people in rain forests make[a] living is by practicing *slash-and-burn agriculture.* Slash-and-burn farmers crea[te] fields for their crops by cutting down patches of forest, letting the vegetation dry f[or] a while, and then clearing the "slash" by burning it. At first, the ash left by the fi[re] makes a nutrient-rich bed for crops. But a field loses its fertility within a few yea[rs,] and a farmer eventually abandons it and clears another patch of forest.

Today slash-and-burn agriculture, as it's practiced by the huge numbers of s[et]tlers that are moving into rain forests, is a major cause of tropical deforestation [in] some areas. Yet many indigenous (native) peoples, such as the Lua' of Thaila[nd] and the Maya of Central America, have been practicing slash-and-burn agricultu[re] for hundreds of years without destroying their rain forest homes.

Jungle Traditions: Many indigenous farmers in rain forests are subsisten[ce] farmers: They raise food for their families and/or their communities, and they us[u]ally don't sell much (if any) of what they harvest. These farmers typically live [in] small communities of several families, and they cultivate small areas near their v[il]

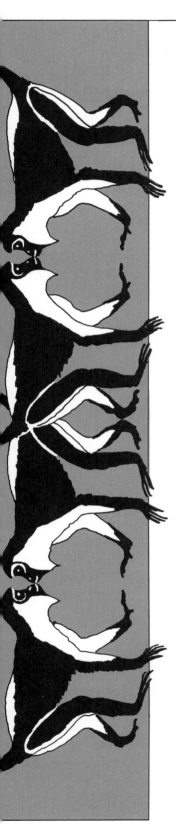

lage using slash-and-burn techniques. After farming a plot for several years, these indigenous farmers have traditionally let the cultivated area lie fallow for about 20 years or more before cultivating it again. In the meantime they work other fields near the village, letting them lie fallow in their turn.

During the fallow years, a relatively small agricultural field can revert to jungle. And when the plot is eventually cut and burned the next time, the nutrients that have accumulated in the growing vegetation again become available for crops.

The Old Ways and the New: Because their populations are low and because they let their fields lie fallow for a long time after cultivation, indigenous farmers have historically been able to practice slash-and-burn agriculture without permanently destroying the land. Their use of the rain forest, in other words, is *sustainable*. On the other hand, the huge numbers of people currently moving into rain forests from overcrowded cities and other areas are causing permanent and widespread damage to rain forests. That's because they're collectively slashing and burning huge areas of land. And the cleared areas usually aren't allowed to lie fallow for very long before they're cultivated again or before they're converted to cattle pasture. (See "The New Settlers" on page 48 for more about deforestation caused by slash-and-burn farming.).

Hunting for a Living: Some people that live in rain forests focus their energies more on hunting meat and collecting wild plant food than they do on agriculture. A few of these *hunter-gatherers* do grow one or more crops, and some get their plant food from neighboring farmers by trading wild meat or field labor for fresh fruits and vegetables. But many hunter-gatherers get most of the food they need directly from the wild.

Relying primarily on hunting and gathering to make a living isn't as widespread a method of surviving in the rain forest as farming. But hunter-gatherers do live here and there in rain forests around the world. The Mbuti pygmies of central Africa are rain forest hunter-gatherers, as are the Agta of the Philippines. Like indigenous rain forest farmers, these and other hunter-gatherers live in relatively small groups that the jungle can easily accommodate.

For the most part, rain forest hunter-gatherers live pretty much as their ancestors did generations ago. They hunt with spears, blowguns, or bows and arrows, or they catch game in traps, nets, or snares. And they use wild plants not only for food, but also to treat illnesses and, depending on the group, to make everything from hammocks to houses.

"Odd" Jobs: For many people who live in tropical rain forests, the classifications of "subsistence farmer" or "hunter-gatherer" either don't really apply or are just too narrow. Rain forests are home to a lot of different peoples—many of whom aren't indigenous to the area—and they've found a lot of different ways of making a living. For example, many rain forest residents farm, hunt, and fish not only to feed their families, but also to sell goods to outside buyers. Other forest people earn an income by tapping rubber and/or by collecting palm hearts, Brazil nuts, or other jungle commodities.

(continued next page)

FORESTS FULL OF RICHES

People who live and work in rain forests have much to offer the rest of the world. From indigenous jungle farmers, we might be able to learn more about sustainable agriculture in the rain forest. We also stand to gain a lot from the people who gather and use wild rain forest plants. The rain forest's incredible diversity means that there's a lot of potential for adding medicines, foods, and other rain forest products to the already rich supply of jungle-derived goods. And the shamans of indigenous rain forest tribes represent a collective storehouse of botanical knowledge.

The Race to Learn: Scientists are trying to learn as much as they can about indigenous people and how they use their environment. In fact, the field of *ethnobotany* has gained momentum in recent years, the result of a desire to understand how jungle plants might benefit the rest of the world. (Ethnobotany is the study of how indigenous people use local plants.)

Most rain forest ethnobotanists go about their work with a sense of urgency. Rain forests are quickly disappearing, and the shamans are dying out. Traditional values and ways of life are slipping away from indigenous people as modern culture infiltrates their rain forest homes—and there aren't many young tribal members learning about the old ways. (For information about cultural loss, displacement, and extinction of native peoples, see "Human Costs" on page 49.)

Jungle Connections: Jungle products—many of which were introduced to scientists and explorers by indigenous people—have affected us in a lot of far-reaching ways. Some have even helped to save lives. Curare, for example, comes from the resins of certain jungle vines. Physicians use a synthesized version of curare as a muscle relaxant for patients undergoing abdominal surgery. (For generations, some native tribes have coated the tips of arrows and blowgun darts with curare. The curare-tipped weapons paralyze the muscles of prey animals, making the wounded animals easier to catch.)

Some jungle commodities also have potential in areas besides the ones in which they're already being used. The oil found in Brazil's copaiba tree, for example, has been used as a perfume base. But recent research suggests that it might also make a great diesel engine fuel and could become an alternative energy source in the future. (For more about rain forest products, see "Jungle in the Pantry" on page 41.)

A Stake in the Future: Besides being good for people, new jungle products could be good for the jungle too—*if* they're properly managed. For example, a plant containing a cure for cancer might be protected once it was discovered. And its rain forest habitat might be protected too—at least until people found a way to cultivate the plant or until the plant's chemical compounds could be synthesized in labs. Even then, wild strains of the original plant could be valuable in developing better domestic versions, just as wild varieties of certain crops are used to make existing crops hardier.

A newly discovered jungle fruit or other food, given a niche in the marketplace, could get special treatment too. That's what happened with the Brazil nut tree, which is difficult to cultivate. Because the people who gather Brazil nuts for sale—as well as those who buy the nuts—have a stake in the welfare of Brazil nut trees, certain areas where the trees grow have been given some protection.

In many ways, some of which we don't even understand yet, all of us have a stake in the welfare of tropical rain forests and of the people, wildlife, and plants that live in them. See chapter 4 for information about how and why rain forests are being destroyed, the role that rain forests are thought to play in maintaining the health of the planet, and some ways people are working to solve the problems that these forests are facing.

Forest People

Objective:
Describe the lifestyle of an indigenous tropical rain forest culture.

Ages:
Primary

Materials:
copies of page 45
story on page 38
scissors
crayons or markers
globe or world map
pictures of pygmies (optional)
glue (optional)
construction paper (optional)

Subjects:
Social Studies and Geography

Tucked away from modern civilization in isolated pockets of jungle are forest people who live much as their ancestors have for thousands of years. By listening to a story about an African pygmy family, your kids can find out how one group of rain forest people lives.

Begin the activity by showing the kids where they live on a globe or world map. Next point to the northeast corner of Zaire (in the central part of Africa). Tell the kids that in this spot there's a large area of jungle called the Ituri (ih-TUR-ee) Forest where people called pygmies live. (See the map on page 39.) If possible, show the kids some pictures of pygmies. Discuss the general conditions in a tropical rain forest. Then explain that the forest is very important to the pygmies' way of life.

Now pass out a copy of page 45 to each child. Have the kids cut the pictures apart.

Then have them look at the pictures while you read "People of the Forest" on page 38. The story describes how a pygmy boy named Kebe (KEH-bay) and his little sister Alita (ah-LEE-ta) live with their family in the African rain forest. (You can pause at each place that describes one of the pictures and have the kids point to the appropriate one. Pauses are marked in the story with an asterisk.)

When you've finished reading the story, have the kids compare how their own families live with the way Kebe and Alita's family lives. (Use the information under "Pygmies of the Ituri" on page 39 to help with your discussion.) For example, you can ask the kids some of these questions:

1. Find the picture that shows Ima (EE-mah), Kebe and Alita's mother, building a hut. How is the hut like your house? How is it different? Did your family build your house? Do pygmy families live alone or near other families? Do you live near other families? Has your family ever moved? If so, why? Why do groups of pygmies move from place to place?

2. Find the picture that shows Kebe and his father Alukulu (ah-LOO-koo-loo), hunting. Why do the pygmies hunt? What is one kind of animal they hunt? How does your family get its food?

3. Find the picture that shows Alita helping her mother gather food and firewood. What kinds of foods do the pygmies gather? Do you eat any of the same kinds of foods they eat? What chores do you do to help your family?

4. Find the picture that shows Kebe breaking into the bee hive for honey. Do you ever eat honey? What other special foods do you like to eat?

After your discussion, have the children color their pictures. You may want to have them glue the pictures onto pieces of construction paper to make a storybook about Kebe and Alita. *(continued next page)*

David S. Wilkie

Deep in the African jungle, Kebe (KEH-bay) and his sister Alita (ah-LEE-ta) were traveling with their parents and several other families. They were looking for a place in the forest to build a new camp.

Finally, in a clearing near a small stream, the group stopped to set up camp. There was much to do. First each family needed a new hut. Ima (EE-mah), Kebe and Alita's mother, cut young trees and used them to make their hut. She bent the trees and wove them into a dome-shaped frame. Then she covered the frame with big leaves. The finished huts of all the families formed a circle in the clearing, with all the doorways facing toward the center. ✳

Kebe and Alita's father, Alukulu (ah-LOO-koo-loo), worked with the other men. They were making sure their bowstrings were tight and strong for the hunt the next day. Alukulu had told Kebe that he could join them on the hunt. Kebe was so excited, he could hardly wait.

When the sun came up the next morning, Kebe was the first one ready. The other boys and the men finally gathered their bows and arrows, and they all set off into the forest. Kebe knew they would probably find some small antelopes called duikers (DYE-kerz). The pygmies hunted other animals too, but most of the meat they ate came from these small, deerlike creatures.

After they'd been walking for a while, Alukulu and several other men moved ahead, formed a half-circle, and quietly waited. Then Kebe and the others spread out and began to march through the forest toward the waiting men with bows, beating the brush and shouting. The noise frightened animals straight toward the hunters, who shot them with their arrows. On the first try, Alukulu's arrow hit a duiker. Kebe was proud of his father's skill. ✳

The hunters repeated their technique several times in other areas of the forest. Then they cut all the meat up, wrapped it in leaves, and divided it among themselves.

On their way back to camp, the hunters also collected other food, such as tortoises, fruit, birds' eggs, and even termites, snails, and caterpillars. As they walked, Alukulu noticed that many bees were going in and out of a

hive high in the trunk of a huge tree. He knew that before too many days had passed, the group would be able to collect a special treat: honey.

While the men were out hunting, the women had been busy too. Although the men and boys in the group hunted for meat and gathered some other foods, it was the women and girls who gathered most of the foods the pygmies ate, as well as the firewood they used for cooking the meals. Alita and all the girls and women in the group had important jobs, such as preparing the food, carrying water from the stream, and caring for small children. ✳

Each day Ima, Alita, and the other women and girls searched for nuts, berries, mushrooms, roots, and firewood. Alita had made her own little basket and used it to help collect what she found.

Ima and Alita had gathered plenty of food for a good meal that night. When the hunters returned and Kebe brought their share of the duiker meat, Ima was pleased to add it to the other foods in her cookpot.

After the evening feast, the families gathered around the fires to chat. Then the men told the story of their hunt. Soon everyone began to sing and dance. Some people also played drums and other musical instruments. Many of the pygmies danced late into the night. But Kebe and Alita were

David S. Wilkie

both exhausted from the day's work. They soon fell fast asleep, despite the noisy celebration.

Many days later, Alukulu decided it was the right time to collect honey from the bee hive he had found earlier. He led Kebe and some of the men to the honey tree. Kebe could climb trees like an expert, so he was chosen to raid the hive. Alukulu handed him a big knife and a leaf basket filled with burning bits of wood.

Kebe climbed high into the tree until he finally reached the hive. The smoke from the burning wood calmed the bees. He began to hit the tree trunk with his knife. Whack! Whack! Whack! ✳

Finally Kebe broke into the hive. He reached in and pulled out some of the honeycomb. Some of the bees stung him, but it was worth it—the honey tasted so good! Kebe threw down pieces of honeycomb, and the men caught them in huge leaves they held up. The men ate their fill. Then they took the extra honeycomb back to camp for the rest of the group to enjoy.

While the men and boys were collecting honey, the women and girls had been busy gathering food near the camp. Alita had decided to look for something special. She knew that opi (OH-pee) fruit ripened at the same time of year that the men collected honey. And she knew there was absolutely nothing better than opi fruit dipped in honey!

While Ima was collecting some mushrooms, Alita had wandered off a little way until she came to one of the tall, straight opi trees where lots of the dark fruit had fallen to the ground. She had filled her basket full of the olivelike fruit, then ran quickly back to show her mother. Ima was proud of Alita. When Alita told everyone where the tree was, other families went to collect more opi fruit. What a treat they all had!

As the days passed, the pygmy group found less and less to eat near their camp. That meant that it was time to move on. Once again, Kebe and Alita's family walked off with the others to find a new place in the forest to camp. Kebe and Alita didn't have much to carry with them. They knew that the forest would provide whatever they needed.

Deep in the Forest: Much of the Congo River basin in Zaire is relatively isolated and undisturbed. This part of equatorial Africa, which includes the Ituri Forest, represents a major portion of what's left of the world's tropical rain forests.

Forest People: Pygmies are one of various cultural groups that live in central Africa. Their characteristic reddish-brown skin and small stature (they're about 4—4 1/2 feet tall) are two features that make pygmies unique. Although there are several different groups of pygmies, the story in this activity describes a subgroup of Mbuti (mm-BOO-tee) pygmies called the Efe (EH-fay).

Finding Food: The Efe are hunter-gatherers, foraging for food in the wild instead of raising their own. Some associate with other groups that live in villages and cultivate crops. Though the Efe may work in their fields and trade meat and honey for cultivated foods and other goods, they've maintained their cultural identity. They are basically nomadic people, traveling from place to place as the forest's food supply fluctuates.

What's for Dinner? The Efe are opportunists who take advantage of whatever the forest has to offer, whenever it's available. Occasionally they hunt large game, such as elephants, okapi, and buffalo. But they mostly hunt duikers, and sometimes monkeys, rodents, and birds. The women provide well over half of the food the Efe eat, either by collecting it in the forest or by working for it in villages.

The Efe especially look forward to honey season. The incredible amount of honey the Efe consume during this brief season makes up a substantial portion of their total yearly calorie intake.

The Hunt: The Efe are bow-and-arrow hunters, and only the men and boys hunt. Sometimes hunting is a cooperative effort, as described in the story, and sometimes individual men hunt on their own. (Another group of Mbuti pygmies uses nets to hunt, and men, women, and children all participate.)

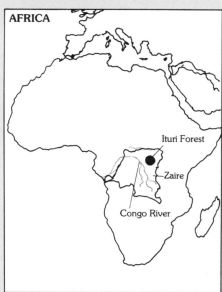

AFRICA

Ituri Forest

Zaire

Congo River

A Way of Life: The Efe live in fairly small bands of several families. All the people in the camp share chores. But in general, the men hunt and collect honey, while the women fish, build huts, collect wood and water, gather and prepare food, and take care of children. Efe children develop "adult" skills as they play. Girls become skilled at their chores from about age three on, and boys begin hunting at about age nine or ten.

The Forest as Provider: The forest provides everything the Efe need to survive. It provides not only their food, but also their clothing in the form of bark, which they hammer into cloth and paint. The forest also shelters the Efe from the elements and provides materials for their homes.

The Efe keep very few possessions. They simply take what they need to survive from the forest. Their impact on the forest is minimal because their numbers are few and because they don't stay in any one place for very long.

Tropical Treats

ry some tropical rain
rest recipes.

bjective:
dentify some common
ods that originated in
opical rain forests.

ges:
rimary, Intermediate,
d Advanced

aterials:
See individual reci-
pes for ingredients
and utensils.
copies of page 46

ubject:
cience

Your group can have fun preparing a tropical feast. And they'll be surprised to learn how many of our common foods originated in tropical rain forests. If you're working with older kids, you may want to try "Jungle in the Pantry" on page 41 first. You can also bring in a few of the food products listed on page 46 for the kids to sample. Then try some of the recipes on the next page. The tropical forest ingredients in each recipe are printed in italics. *(continued next page)*

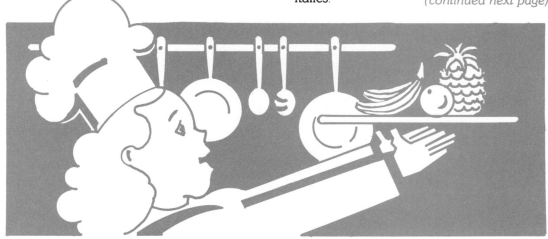

Make copies of the list of food products on page 46 and give one to each child. Have the kids use their lists to plan a menu for one day's meals, using as many tropical forest foods as possible. For example, breakfast might consist of toast sprinkled with cinnamon and sugar, a grapefruit half, and a cup of hot chocolate. The sugar, cinnamon, grapefruit, and cocoa orig- inated in tropical forests. (You can have younger kids take their lists home and work out their menus with their parents. Suggest that the children actually prepare and eat their tropical meals.

Discuss some of the menus the children came up with, making sure they point out the tropical forest ingredients. You may want to combine all their ideas, along with the recipes provided in this activity, to make a group book of tropical treats. Then you can make copies of the book so each child can have one to take home.

Jungle Punch

1 banana
1 cup orange juice
1 cup pineapple juice
1 can lemon-lime soda
1 pint lemon sherbet

Puree a soft, ripe banana in a blender. Add the orange juice and pineapple juice and blend to- gether. Just before serving, add the lemon-lime soda and mix well. Put a spoonful of lemon sherbet in each glass and fill with punch. Makes about 1 quart.

Tropical Trail Mix

1 cup cashew pieces
1 cup peanuts
1 cup broken banana chips
1 cup chocolate chips
1 cup dried pineapple chunks
½ cup coconut flakes

Combine the ingredients in a large mixing bowl. Makes about 2 pounds. *Note:* You may want to add other tropical items if you can find them. Some possibilities include sesame seeds, Brazil nuts, dried papaya, and macadamia nuts.

Rain Forest Chip Dip

1 avocado
1 tablespoon lemon juice
1 small tomato
1 tablespoon grated onion
½ teaspoon salt
¼ teaspoon chili powder
3 tablespoons mayonnaise
dash paprika
corn chips

Mash a soft, ripe avocado in a small bowl. Thoroughly mix in the lemon juice. Chop the tomato and add to the mixture. Blend in the on- ion, salt, chili powder, and mayonnaise. Sprinkle with paprika and serve with corn chips. Makes about 1 cup. *Note:* If you're making the dip ahead of time, spread the mayonnaise in a layer over the avocado mixture and refrigerate. Then blend in the mayonnaise when ready to serve. This will help prevent the avocado from discolor- ing.

South-of-the-Border Chocolate

⅓ cup cocoa
½ cup sugar
1 tablespoon instant decaffeinated coffee
¼ teaspoon cinnamon
1 quart milk
1 teaspoon vanilla
whipped topping
nutmeg

In a saucepan, heat the milk until it's hot, but not boiling. Mix together the cocoa, sugar, coffee, and cinnamon in a small bowl. Add 2 table- spoons of the hot milk to the chocolate mixture and stir the mixture until it's smooth. Blend the chocolate mixture into the remaining milk. Re- move from heat, add vanilla, and beat the mix- ture with a wire whisk until it's frothy. To serve, fill cups with the hot chocolate, add a spoonful of whipped topping to each, and sprinkle with nut- meg. Makes about 1 quart.

Jungle in the Pantry

Search for household items that come from tropical forests, and then research their origins.

Objective:
Name some common products that originated in tropical forests.

Ages:
Intermediate and Advanced

Materials:
• *copies of page 46*
• *reference books*
• *paper and pencils*

Subjects:
Science and Social Studies

TROPICAL PRODUCTS

bamboo
banana
chicle (chewing gum)
chocolate
coconut
coffee
cola (kola nut)
curare
jute
orange
pepper
pineapple
quinine
rattan
rubber
tropical hardwoods (teak, mahogany)
vanilla

Y ou may have heard the expression, "It's a jungle out there!" But you may not realize that there's probably a "jungle" in your own home too. Many of the products that we use every day have their origins in tropical forests.

In this two-part activity, your group will have a chance to discover which of these products are in their own homes. Then they'll do some research to find out more about where these products come from. But before you start, copy each of the products listed in the margin onto a slip of paper and put the slips aside.

PART 1: JUNGLE PRODUCT SURVEY

Begin this part of the activity by going over what tropical rain forests are and where they're located, using the background information on pages 3–5 and the map on pages 18 and 19. Then ask the kids if they can think of anything they use that might have come from a tropical rain forest. Tell them that many of the things we use every day originated in tropical forests. You may want to bring in samples of some of the products listed on page 46.

Pass out a copy of page 46 to each person and go over the product lists. Explain that all the products on the page originated in tropical forests. (*Note:* Most of these products originated in tropical rain forests, but we have included several important products—marked with an asterisk—that may have gotten their start in other types of tropical habitats near rain forests. And the plants these products

originated from could be affected by the destruction of rain forests.)

Next use the information under "Tropical Wealth" on the next page to describe the general types of products that have come from tropical forests. Then have the kids take their lists home and work with their parents to see how many of the products they can find. Tell them to check off each item they find. (Also have them circle items they know they've had in the house before, but currently don't have.) The items in parentheses should give the kids some ideas of where to look.

When the kids return with their completed checklists, use the results and the background information on page 36 to discuss the importance of tropical rain forests in our daily lives. Explain that many of the products on the list, such as citrus fruits, are now cultivated and harvested in other parts of the world. And, in some cases, synthetic alternatives, such as artificial flavors and synthetic rubber, have been developed to replace certain jungle products.

But some of the products still come directly from tropical forests. Mention that the demand for some of these products, such as tropical hardwoods, has contributed to the destruction of tropical rain forests. Explain that for people to continue to enjoy and benefit from tropical resources, we must harvest them carefully and use them wisely. Unless people protect tropical forest ecosystems, we may never know about many other potential products. (For more about the problems of tropical deforestation, see chapter 4.)

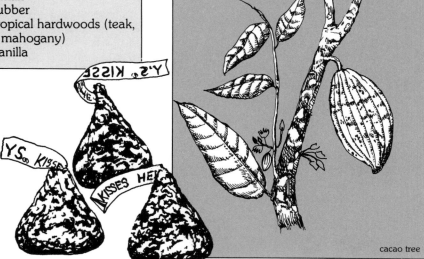
cacao tree

Now the kids can find out more about some of these tropical forest products. Divide your group into pairs and have each pair draw one of the product slips you made earlier. Then have the pairs research the products they drew.

Encourage the kids to talk to people who may know more about their products. For example, a pharmacist may be able to give more information about tropical medicines.

Here are some research questions the kids should try to answer:

1. What plant does your product come from? What does the plant look like, and what part of the plant is used?

2. Do/did native people use your product? If so, how? Do other people use your product now? If so, how?

3. How/when was your product discovered by non-native people?

4. If your product has to be processed or manufactured, what is the procedure?

5. Where in the tropics did your product originally come from? Is the plant now cultivated somewhere other than where it originated? If so, where?

6. Are there any substitutes for your product? If so, what are they?

After the kids have finished their research, have them present their information to the whole group. Also have them include a picture of the plant their product comes from, if possible, and bring in a sample or a picture of their product.

After the presentations, the kids can set up a "tropical treasures" display in one area of the room, featuring their reports, drawings, and samples. They can add labeled samples of some of the other products listed on page 46 too.

TROPICAL WEALTH

Woods, Canes, and Fibers: Some of the world's most beautiful woods, including teak and mahogany, come from tropical forest trees. People use tropical hardwoods for construction, for boats, and for furniture and many other household products.

Tropical fibers are important in making packaging materials and cording and also for soundproofing and insulation. People use the fibers and stems of different species of palms to make woven goods, such as baskets, mats, cane chair seats, window blinds, hats, and knit fabrics.

Foods: Try to imagine life without coffee or chocolate! These and other foods we eat, as well as many of the flavors we use to enhance our foods, come directly from tropical forests. Some tropical foods and spices, though, originated in certain forests, but are now also grown in other tropical areas. Bananas, for instance, got their start in Malaysia, but Brazil is now the leading banana producer.

Wild relatives of some of the world's staple crops still grow in tropical areas. These wild strains are im-

portant to agriculture because they can be crossed with cultivated varieties to help keep these domestic crops strong and healthy. There are potentially many other food sources in tropical forests too.

Gums, Resins, and Oils: The saps and other juices of some tropical plants are important components in a number of products. Rubber, derived from latex in trees in Amazonia, is probably the most well-known product. (Rubber trees are now grown in Southeast Asia.) Another latex is tapped from sapodilla trees in Central America to produce chicle, a substance that's been used to make chewing gum. And tree resins such as copal and dammar are used to make varnishes, enamels, and lacquers.

Some oils are distilled from different parts of trees, such as the fruits (lime), flowers (ylang-ylang), leaves (bay), or wood (sandalwood). The pharmaceutical and cosmetic industries use these oils for their medicinal properties or for their flavor and/or scent. People use other oils, such as coconut and palm, for cooking. Some

of these oils are also used in making soaps, candles, and lotions.

Houseplants: Many of the evergreen plants that grow in tropical rain forests also grow very successfully indoors as houseplants. Common houseplants that originated in tropical rain forests include African violets and many species of orchids and bromeliads.

Other Tropical Forest Products: Some tanning substances and dyes are derived from tropical plants. For example, annatto is an orange-red dye that comes from the seeds of a small tree. It's been used to color fabrics, foods, cosmetics, and polishes. Rotenone, a poisonous substance that comes from the roots of the *Derris* plant, is commonly used as an insecticide.

Many important drugs are also derived from tropical plants. Here's a look at a few:

● *curare*—derived from a tropical vine; native peoples use it as a poison on darts and arrows; doctors use a synthesized version as a muscle relaxant during surgery

- *ipecac*—made from the roots of a Brazilian plant; used to treat dysentery and as an emetic
- *quinine*—made from the bark of the *Cinchona* tree; used to prevent and treat malaria and also used in carbonated beverages
- *reserpine*—derived from *Rauvolfia* plants; used in treating hypertension
- *vincristine*—derived from the rosy periwinkle of Madagascar; used to treat Hodgkin's disease and childhood leukemia.

Pets: Tropical birds have been a part of people's lives for a long time. For example, most experts think the ancestor of our domestic chicken is the jungle fowl of Southeast Asia. And for centuries, people have kept many kinds of brightly colored tropical birds as pets—notably the parrots.

Many reptiles from tropical forests, such as iguanas, chameleons, boas, and caimans, end up in the pet trade too. And tropical aquarium fish, such as swordtails and certain tetras and angelfish, originated in rain forest rivers and streams.

Although many of these animals are raised in captivity, far too many are smuggled from the wild. (For more about the illegal wildlife trade, see chapter 3 of *Nature-Scope—Endangered Species: Wild and Rare.*)

Treetop Explorers

Design a method for exploring the rain forest canopy.

Objectives:
Describe some of the characteristics of a rain forest canopy. Discuss several ways to study the canopy.

Ages:
Advanced

Materials:
copies of page 47
pictures of a tropical rain forest and tropical rain forest plants and animals
drawing paper
markers or crayons

Subject:
Science

There's a hidden world in tropical treetops that scientists have only recently begun to investigate. In this activity, your group will develop strategies for exploring this vast frontier.

To start the activity, show the kids pictures of a tropical rain forest and some of the plants and animals that live there. If possible, point out species that spend most of their lives in the treetops. (See "Canopy Critters" on page 24 for some examples of animals that live in the canopy.) Then describe the canopy, using the information in "The Canopy—Treetops of Life" on page 4. Explain that scientists still know relatively little about this sky-high habitat because it's mostly out of sight and out of reach. But some people have devised ways to make the canopy a little more accessible. Tell the kids that they'll have a chance to devise some of their own ways of studying the canopy.

Now divide your group into teams of two or three kids. Pass out a copy of page 47 to each child. Tell the kids to read over the facts, which describe pollination and conditions in the rain forest canopy. (You may want to review pollination with the kids.)

Have the kids pretend that their team is a team of scientists interested in researching the pollination of a kind of plant that blooms in the tropical rain forest canopy. Tell the kids that they know what this plant's flowers look like. They also know

that the flowers are pollinated by animals, but they don't know if the pollinators are one species of animal or several different species. And they don't know how the flowers attract the pollinators or when the flowers bloom. Explain that their team's goals are:
1. to decide what they need to know in order to find out what animal or animals pollinate the flowers, and
2. to figure out how they would conduct their research.

To get started, have team members brainstorm some general ideas. Tell the kids to keep in mind how they might be able to observe the flowers and the animals that visit them in such a high environment, how much time they might need to spend observing them, and what type of equipment they might need. Have them choose a method they think would work best, and then draw a diagram to illustrate it.

Be sure to explain that there's no one "right" way to study something that lives in the canopy. The important thing is for the kids to work together and use relevant information from their fact sheet to come up with some ways that seem reasonable.

When the kids have finished their discussions, have a spokesperson for each team describe his or her team's exploration method, supporting it with relevant facts from the Copycat Page and showing their drawing. Then have the whole group discuss the pros and cons of each design.

Afterward use the information under "The Climb to the Top" below to go over some of the actual methods scientists have devised to get into the treetops of tropical rain forests. Then have the kids compare these methods with the ones they designed.

THE CLIMB TO THE TOP

Monkey Business: Some animal trainers in Southeast Asia teach macaques—a kind of monkey—to pick coconuts from tall palms. One scientist retrained some of these monkeys to twist off small branches from tall trees so he could study the leaves and flowers on them.

Room with a View: Some scientists have made studies from an observation tower built alongside tall rain forest trees. One scientist would like to try computer-controlled video cameras to get an even closer look. These cameras would be suspended from cables between towers and could zoom in on any part of the canopy.

Chop, Shoot, or Spray 'Em Down: Some people have collected specimens of canopy plants and animals by chopping down tall trees, by shooting down birds and mammals, or by blasting down high limbs with a shotgun. Some biologists spray an insect-killing fog into the canopy and then collect the insects that fall. Of course, these methods are more damaging than many others, and scientists are very careful about how they conduct these studies.

Tree People: Some scientists wear spiked shoes and harnesses for climbing tall trees. Others drive metal bolts into the trunk to have something to grab onto or to step on. These methods are not widely used because they can injure trees by damaging their bark.

Rope Climbers: Some scientists use a harness and special clamps to inch their way slowly up a rope—a technique many mountain climbers use. First they use a crossbow, catapult, or gun to fire a nylon line over a high limb. Then they tie a rope to the line, pull the line with the rope attached to it over the limb, and secure the rope so they can climb it.

Precarious Platforms: Once a scientist has climbed to the canopy, he or she can set up a "tree house" in the branches. This is usually just a platform with a sloped, plastic ceiling to protect the scientist and equipment from the rain. The scientist can spend long periods on this platform, quietly studying the surroundings.

Spiderman: One scientist uses a triangular rope web stretched across the canopy. Sitting in a kind of harness attached to the rope by a wheel, he can move to any point in the web.

Canopy Crane: Scientists are trying out a new canopy access system in Panama that uses a construction crane. The crane supports a gondola that holds a scientist and equipment. The scientist can move the gondola to reach heights of up to 180 feet, or out in a 525-foot-wide circle.

Floating on Air: Planes and helicopters could scan the tops of trees, but they're expensive to operate and create too much wind and noise. One scientist drifted gently over the treetops in a hot air balloon attached to a large, lightweight platform. Once the platform was lowered onto the canopy and tied down, the balloon was deflated, and the scientist could explore the canopy.

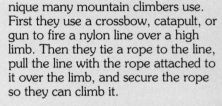

WOODS, CANES, AND FIBERS

Woods
(furniture, floors, doors, paneling, cabinets, carvings, toys, models)
- ___ balsa
- ___ mahogany
- ___ rosewood
- ___ sandalwood
- ___ teak*

Canes and Fibers
- ___ bamboo (cane furniture, crafts)
- ___ jute* (rope, twine, burlap)
- ___ kapok (insulation, stuffing)
- ___ ramie* (knit materials)
- ___ rattan (furniture, wicker, cane chair seats)

FOOD PRODUCTS

Fruits and Vegetables
- ___ avocado
- ___ banana
- ___ grapefruit
- ___ guava
- ___ heart of palm
- ___ lemon
- ___ lime
- ___ mango
- ___ orange
- ___ papaya
- ___ passion fruit
- ___ pepper
- ___ pineapple
- ___ plantain
- ___ potato*
- ___ sweet potato*
- ___ tangerine
- ___ tomato*
- ___ yam*

Spices and Flavors
- ___ allspice
- ___ black pepper
- ___ cardamom
- ___ cayenne (red pepper)
- ___ chili pepper
- ___ chocolate or cocoa
- ___ cinnamon
- ___ cloves
- ___ ginger
- ___ mace
- ___ nutmeg
- ___ paprika
- ___ turmeric
- ___ vanilla

Other Food Products
- ___ Brazil nuts
- ___ cashew nuts
- ___ coconut
- ___ coffee
- ___ corn*
- ___ macadamia nuts
- ___ peanuts*
- ___ rice*
- ___ sesame seeds*
- ___ sugar*
- ___ tapioca
- ___ tea

HOUSEHOLD PRODUCTS

Houseplants
- ___ African violet
- ___ aluminum plant
- ___ *Begonia*
- ___ bird's-nest fern
- ___ bromeliads
- ___ Christmas cactus
- ___ *Croton*
- ___ *Dracaena*
- ___ dumb cane (*Dieffenbachia*)
- ___ fiddle-leaf fig
- ___ kentia palm
- ___ orchids
- ___ *Philodendron*
- ___ prayer plant
- ___ rubber plant
- ___ snake plant (*Sansevieria*)
- ___ spathe lily
- ___ swiss-cheese plant
- ___ umbrella tree (*Schefflera*)
- ___ zebra plant (*Aphelandra*)

Oils
- ___ bay (bay rum lotion)
- ___ camphor (insect repellent, medicine)
- ___ coconut (snack food, baked goods, lotions, soap)
- ___ lime (food flavoring, candles, soap, bath oil)
- ___ palm (snack food, baked goods)
- ___ patchouli (perfume, soap)
- ___ rosewood (perfume)
- ___ sandalwood (soap, candles, perfume)

Gums and Resins
- ___ chicle (chewing gum)
- ___ copal (varnish, printing ink)
- ___ dammar (varnish, lacquer)
- ___ rubber (balloons, erasers, foam rubber, balls, rubber bands, rubber cement, gloves, hoses, shoes, tires)

* products that may have originated in other types of tropical habitats near rain forests

The sun and wind are stronger and the rainfall is heavier in the canopy than on the forest floor.

Weather conditions can change quickly and drastically in a tropical rain forest.

To best understand how plants and animals live, scientists must study them in their natural habitats.

Animals can be frightened by unfamiliar things in their habitat. It takes time for them to get used to a scientist studying them.

The highest branches of the canopy can be more than 100 feet above the ground. (That's higher than a 10-story building!)

The lowest branches of all trees can be more than 30 feet above the ground.

Many canopy flowers bloom at the outer fringes of the crowns of trees.

Animals that commonly pollinate rain forest flowers include many kinds of insects, birds, and bats.

Many flowers have adaptations that attract certain pollinators. For example, flowers with different shapes, colors, and odors are pollinated by different kinds of animals.

PROBLEMS AND SOLUTIONS

Deforestation in the tropics isn't a straightforward problem that can [be] traced to just one or two sources. It's the result of a combination [of] social, political, and economic problems, and it's aggravated by t[he] special characteristics of tropical topography, soils, and other physic[al] features. And the effects of deforestation are as complex as the causes. Findi[ng] solutions to this sticky web of issues is proving to be a major challenge—but it's [a] challenge we won't be able to ignore.

SOME CAUSES AND CONSEQUENCES

Rain Forest Ranching: Since the 1950s, when the push to make the jung[le] "useful" started to accelerate, millions of acres of rain forest—mostly in Centr[al] and South America—have been converted to cattle pasture. Corporations, as w[ell] as individual landholders, are responsible for most of the ranching that takes pla[ce] in the tropics.

Although conversion to pasture is a popular use of rain forest land, it's definite[ly] not a sustainable one in most areas. At first, the nutrients released when a patch [of] forest is burned result in lush grasslands—but tropical downpours, along with t[he] pounding of cattle's hooves, soon erode the thin soil. More often than not, t[he] pasture eventually ends up gullied, ravaged, and unable to support anything but [a] few weeds or shrubs.

The New Settlers: Before they're used as pasture, many areas of former ra[in] forest serve time as slash-and-burn fields. Slash-and-burn agriculture is a commo[n] method of farming in the tropics—and if it's practiced carefully, it *can* be sustai[n]able. (See pages 34 and 35 for information on how indigenous rain forest farme[rs] use slash-and-burn methods without destroying the forest.) But it becomes [a] problem when too many people practice it in too small of an area, and when t[he] techniques they use aren't suited to the natural conditions.

Uncontrolled slash-and-burn agriculture is currently eating away at rain fores[t] all over the world. One reason is that more and more people are moving into ju[n]gles, hoping to escape the poverty of overcrowded cities by becoming fronti[er] farmers. And in some cases, people are forced to leave an existing farm whe[n] mechanized agricultural interests take over the land for large-scale cultivation.

Sometimes people are encouraged to move by government resettlement pr[o]grams, which often promise a plot of ground to farm, a house to live in, and oth[er] incentives. And often the roads that are built to give access to resettlement are[as] invite unplanned settlement in places that were once too hard to get to.

In many countries the land that small-scale farmers settle on represents only [a] very small percentage of the country's total land area. The rest of the land is ofte[n] owned by wealthy individuals or corporations. And much of this privately owne[d] land happens to be natural grassland or some other habitat that's better suited f[or] farming than the rain forest land where settlers end up planting their crops.

Tropical Timbers: Logging is an especially big business in the jungles of Afri[ca] and Asia. Typically, a logging operation takes only certain types of trees from t[he] rain forest. But in the tropics individuals of a tree species tend to be few and far b[e]tween, and taking even a few of a certain kind of tree can decimate a species in th[e] area. Just getting to certain trees can be damaging too: Heavy logging equipme[nt] often tears into roots and scrapes into bark, leaving the trees that aren't bei[ng]

jaguar

48

blue-and-yellow
macaw

logged vulnerable to diseases and insect damage. Also, when a giant forest tree is cut, vines connecting it to nearby trees often cause these trees to fall too.

OUTSIDE INFLUENCES

Everyone's Problem: There's no question that rapidly increasing populations in tropical countries often lead to deforestation. Uncontrolled slash-and-burn agriculture is a prime example of how exploding populations and deforestation are connected. But it's unfair to simply blame deforestation on poor families living in tropical countries. Overpopulation is a complex issue that's often caused by (and in turn usually aggravates) poverty.

But some of the influences contributing to deforestation don't originate in the tropics at all. Instead, they often originate in developed countries such as the United States and some European and Asian nations.

Product Demands: The demand in developed countries for rain forest products has a lot to do with why rain forests are disappearing in some areas. Until just a few years ago, for example, consumer demand in the United States for hamburgers at fast-food restaurants formed the basis for much of the Central and South American cattle ranching industry. Pressure from environmental groups, lowered beef consumption, and falling prices of domestic beef have reduced U.S. imports of tropical beef, but some European countries still import a lot of it.

Tropical logging is another example of how the demands of consumers in the developed world can lead to deforestation. Rain forest woods like mahogany and rosewood are in high demand in the United States and other developed countries, where they're used to make furniture and other products.

Short-Sighted Schemes: But the demand for products is only part of the picture. Developed countries also contribute to deforestation by giving financial and political support to certain projects backed by international development banks. These banks have often provided money for the construction of dams, roads, and large-scale agricultural projects. And developing countries, eager to accept projects that they feel will eventually help them pay off their astronomical national debts, encourage the foreign investment.

Ironically, though, development projects financed by banks have often aggravated debt burdens. That's because many of the projects the banks have financed have had disastrous long-term effects that outweigh any short-term gains. While some projects may provide some benefits, such as the electricity generated by a dam, many are basically ill-conceived schemes that benefit relatively few people. And more often than not, the damage done to a rain forest is wide-ranging. For example, clearing an area of its rain forest often causes fragile forest soils to wash into rivers and streams. And this can cause waterways to silt up, making them useless for fishing or transportation.

Human Costs: The environment isn't all that's affected by poorly planned rain forest development. So are indigenous people. Often a tribal group is forced to leave an area the tribe has inhabited for centuries. Many are relocated through government programs—but as settlers move farther into rain forests, many indigenous people are even being pushed out of areas that have been officially designated as native reserves. Unfortunately, governments are often unable—or unwilling—to control the influx of settlers.

(continued next page)

When uncontrolled development pushes into tribal lands, violence often brea out. Settlers, ranchers, and others have killed many indigenous rain forest pe ple—and indigenous people have killed those they view as invaders. Many nati people have also died when exposed to "outsiders' diseases."

FUTURE SHOCK

An Unintentional Experiment: People have manipulated their surroundir since before early humans learned to build fires and wield stone axes. And son times our actions have caused permanent damage to natural habitats. But the ra and scale of the ecological, social, and economic damage we're causing today tropical forests far surpasses anything we've experienced before. And many scie tists think that the long-term effects of tropical deforestation could be much mc devastating and far-reaching than most people expect.

Wasted Potential: Some scientists point to the loss of plant and animal spec as one of the most tragic results of tropical deforestation. Collectively, rain fore are the most diverse habitats on earth—and with every acre of rain forest we cle we're chipping away at that diversity at a rate that some people estimate may be high as six extinctions per hour. Some of the plants, insects, and other spec we're losing are dying out before we even know they exist. By destroying natu diversity, we're not only disrupting natural communities—we're depriving o selves of potential foods, medicines, and other products.

We're also causing changes in the ecology of areas that are nowhere near troy cal forests. Many of "our" familiar songbirds, for example, fly to the tropics for t winter. And some songbird populations have been declining steadily in the pa several years, probably because their winter habitats in tropical areas are disa pearing. A lot of these songbirds feed mostly on insects, and nobody knows y what effect this decline in songbird populations is having on insects in the bird summer habitats. But we *do* know that many of these insects feed on plants, i cluding agricultural crops. So fewer songbirds could mean more insect pes which could ultimately mean more damage to agricultural crops.

Breaking the Cycle: As we carve rain forests into smaller and smaller chun we may also be tampering with weather patterns. Rain forest trees add a lot moisture to the air as excess water evaporates from their leaves, and this moistu eventually falls as rain. Some areas that have been deforested have experienc droughts because the loss of trees disrupted the area's water cycle. And some s entists think that the cumulative effect of tropical deforestation worldwide cou also interfere with global weather patterns.

Deforestation and Global Warming: Many scientists also feel that rain fore destruction may be contributing to the global warming we're experiencing becau of the "greenhouse effect." As rain forests burn, carbon is released from the veg tation and mixes with atmospheric oxygen to form carbon dioxide. Excess carbo dioxide acts like a blanket in the atmosphere, trapping heat against the earth ar ultimately causing the planet to warm up.

HOPE AND HARD WORK

In the News: You may have noticed that rain forests have been in the news late And that's a good sign, even though most of the coverage focuses on tropical d forestation. It's a good sign because it means that people are becoming aware the problems associated with deforestation. And the more we understand wha happening, the better equipped we'll be to find solutions to the problems.

The down side to all the coverage that rain forests are getting is that the negati news tends to overshadow the good news. And there actually *is* some good new Some of the most encouraging projects are local initiatives taking place with

scarlet tanager

Leonard Lee Rue III

tropical rain forest countries. (See "Issues and Answers" on page 58 for more about these local initiatives.) Individuals, governments, and businesses around the world are also working to find solutions to the problem of rain forest destruction.

The Tourist Trade: One of the most effective ways to curb the destruction of tropical rain forests is to provide financial reasons *not* to destroy them. In Costa Rica and other tropical countries, for example, rain forest tourism is a growing business. If it's properly managed, tourism can benefit natural areas by creating an incentive to set up and maintain parks that will attract visitors. Often, international conservation groups, such as the World Wildlife Fund and The Nature Conservancy, provide financial backing for rain forest parks and preserves.

Digging into World Debts: Another financial incentive for preserving tropical rain forests came to light in 1987, when the first debt-for-nature deal was successfully worked out. Briefly, here's how debt-for-nature deals work: A conservation organization or other nonprofit group agrees to buy part of a developing country's debt from a commercial bank. Bank authorities agree to sell the debt at a reduced rate, and the conservation group works out an agreement with both the government of the developing country and a conservation group in that country. Under the terms of the agreement, the developing country makes regular payments to the local conservation organization, which uses the money to help preserve tropical rain forest lands. So far, conservation groups have worked out debt-for-nature swaps in Ecuador, Costa Rica, the Philippines, and other tropical countries.

Improving the Record: There's some good news from international development banks too. Responding to criticism regarding environmentally destructive projects they've financed in the past, some international lending institutions have made efforts to determine, in advance, how their loans will affect tropical rain forests and other habitats. And some, such as the World Bank, have hired environmental advisors who evaluate the environmental impacts of many of the proposals. Certain projects that might once have received funding have recently been turned down by the Bank, on the grounds that they'd cause too many problems. The Bank has also cut off funding for projects when environmental guidelines weren't followed.

Looking Toward the Future: Financial approaches to tropical deforestation, such as the ones mentioned above, are very important since many of the reasons rain forests are being destroyed are based on economics. But there are plenty of people who are approaching the problem from different, and equally important, directions. For example, groups such as the Peace Corps are setting up environmental education programs in tropical countries. Many of these programs are helping local people learn about the rain forest and how to use it sustainably.

And an exciting field of research is gaining momentum these days—the field of habitat restoration. Because of the nature of their soils and other characteristics, tropical rain forests can be nearly impossible to grow from "scratch." But researchers are looking into ways to restore damaged rain forests to a healthier condition. It's just possible that areas thought to be damaged beyond repair will one day be lush again, with huge buttressed trees full of monkeys and parrots and colorful orchids.

We Can All Make a Difference: There's a lot we as individuals can do to help preserve rain forests too. Supporting conservation organizations that focus on rain forests is a good way to start. See page 54 for a partial list of conservation organizations that are working to stop tropical deforestation. And for other ideas on how you and your group can get involved with rain forest protection, see "You Can Help!" on page 52.

magnolia warbler

black-and-white warbler

Art Weber

You Can Help!

Many people assume there's really nothing that anyone in North America can do to help protect tropical rain forests. But that's not true! There *are* projects and programs that you and your kids can get involved in. We've listed a few he but there are many others. You mig want to have your kids brainstorm sor other ways they might be able to he conserve tropical rain forests.

FIVE WAYS TO HELP

1 Learn all you can about tropical rain forests, and then share your knowledge with others. The more people know about tropical rain forests and the problems they are facing, the more likely it is that people will act to help protect them. (See #4 below for project ideas.)

To find out more about tropical rain forests, you can write to Save The Rainforest, a network of about 8500 school groups. It publishes up-to-date information on rain forest issues, offers on-site rain forest courses for teachers and students in Costa Rica and Belize, raises money for rain forest projects worldwide, and coordinates activities with similar networks in Sweden, Japan, and other nations. It also supplies information about specific rain forest projects that school groups can help fund. For more information, write to:
Save The Rainforest
604 Jamie St.
Dodgeville, WI 53533

You can also contact a conservation organization to find out what it's doing to help protect tropical rain forests. (See the partial list on page 54.) Many of these groups sponsor educational programs, fund and conduct research, and help support local initiatives. And many are involved in specific projects to protect certain species or habitats.

2 Write letters to your senators and representatives to let them know that you are concerned about tropical rain forest destruction. Ask that they support programs that help protect tropical rain forests throughout the world. Your group could make the letters more specific by researching a particular problem or country, and then writing a letter based on what they find out.

3 Make personal contact with peop in tropical countries. This will he give your kids a better understanding what life is like in these countries. Y can contact one of the pen pal organiz tions listed below. They may be able help your group exchange letters wi children in other countries. When y write to the pen pal organization, sure to specify several tropical countri that your kids would be interested i Include a business-size self-addresse stamped envelope for the organizatio response. A small fee may be charged.

For ages 6 and up:
International Pen Friends
P.O. Box 65
Brooklyn, NY 11229
(Please include a business-sized, self-addressed, stamped envelope.)

For ages 10 and up:
Student Letter Exchange
630 Third Ave.
New York, NY 10017

People to People International
501 Armour Blvd.
Kansas City, Missouri 64109

4 Raise money to support prograr that are helping to protect the worlc tropical rain forests. Here are some mone raising ideas that can also help others lea more about rain forests:
• Make and sell greeting cards or not cards, on recycled paper, that featu drawings of tropical rain forest plants ar animals. On the backs of the cards, tl kids can include information about tl species shown. (There are many plac

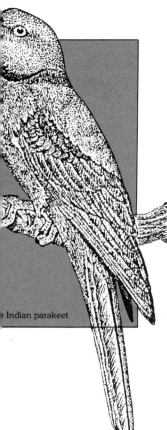

Indian parakeet

that sell recycled paper. Here's one company that produces a catalog of recycled products, including paper supplies: Earth Care Paper, Inc., P.O. Box 14140, Madison, WI 53714.)

- Organize a tropical party or festival, featuring tropical foods, music, and special entertainment. Or hold a tropical treats sale, featuring foods that contain tropical forest ingredients. (See the recipes on page 40 and the tropical products list on page 46 for ideas.)
- Show films or videos about tropical rain forests or species that live in the tropics. You can sell rain forest refreshments at the program. (See page 67 for a list of audiovisual materials.)
- Sponsor a raffle. Try to find a local travel agent or other business that will donate a ticket to a tropical rain forest country and raffle off a trip. Or see if you can get a local food store to donate a tropical food basket for a raffle. Include information about tropical rain forests with each raffle ticket sold.
- Set up a rain forest lecture program, featuring guest speakers who have worked in tropical rain forests. (Check with local universities for possible speakers.) You could charge admission, ask for donations, or sell refreshments.
- Set up a tree-planting program to highlight the problems of tropical deforestation. You can also create an educational display about the effects of worldwide deforestation and try to get local businesses to sponsor your project.
- Organize a "Walk for the Rain Forest." Find local sponsors and citizens to pay for each mile walked and include educational materials about tropical rain forests along the walk site.

5 Support specific projects that are designed to protect tropical rain forests. For example, your group could raise money to help establish "extractive reserves" (see below). We've also included other specific rain forest projects your group can learn more about.

Protecting Rain Forests through "Extractive Reserves"

Harvesting rain forest products while protecting resources and the livelihood of local residents is the idea behind establishing *extractive reserves.* Extractive reserves are large tracts of rain forest set aside for harvesting rubber, Brazil nuts, palm nuts, and other products that grow naturally in rain forests. The harvesting is done in such a way that resources are not destroyed, providing an ongoing source of income for rain forest residents. Clearcutting to support cattle ranching and large-scale agriculture is prohibited on these reserves, but small gardens are encouraged.

By contributing to a special fund set up by the National Wildlife Federation, your group can support the establishment of extractive reserves throughout Amazonia and in other tropical areas of South America. The fund was named for Chico Mendes, a local rubber tapper and ecologist from Brazil who was assassinated in 1988. Mendes led the fight to protect rain forests by showing people that extractive reserves can work. To contribute, make your check out to the National Wildlife Federation and make sure to mark that the money is for the Chico Mendes Fund. Send your check to:

National Wildlife Federation
International Division
Chico Mendes Fund
1400 16th St., NW
Washington, DC 20036-2266

Leapin' Lemurs

Twelve species of lemurs live in the forests of Ranomafana National Park, a newly created wildlife park in Madagascar. Several of these species are endangered or threatened, and scientists are trying to find out more about what they need to survive. These scientists are also working to educate people who live in and near the park about the importance of rain forest protection. For more information about this education and research project, write to:

Duke University Ranomafana Project
c/o Dr. Patricia Wright
Department of Anthropology
Duke University
Durham, NC 27706

Protecting Monkeys and Jaguars

In Belize several wildlife reserves have been established to preserve key habitats for endangered species. Here are two wild-

Organizations Helping to Protect Tropical Forests

Conservation International
1015 18th St., NW
Washington, DC 20036

Global Tomorrow Coalition
1325 G St., NW
Suite 915
Washington, DC 20005

International Union for the
Conservation of Nature
and Natural Resources
Avenue du Mont Blanc
CH-1196 Gland
Switzerland

Missouri Botanical Garden
P.O. Box 299
St. Louis, MO 63166

National Audubon Society
801 Pennsylvania Ave., SE
Washington, DC 20003

National Wildlife
Federation
1400 16th St., NW
Washington, DC 20036-
2266

The Nature Conservancy
1815 North Lynn St.
Arlington, VA 22209

Rainforest Action Network
301 Broadway
Suite A
San Francisco, CA 94133

Smithsonian Tropical
Research Institute
APO
Miami, FL 34002-0011

Wildlife Conservation
International
New York Zoological
Society
Bronx, NY 10460

World Wildlife Fund/
Conservation Foundation
1250 24th St., NW
Washington, DC 20037

---

life reserves that your group can learn more about:

- **Baboon Sanctuary:** The Community Baboon Sanctuary in Belize was established in 1985 to protect one of the few remaining black howler monkey populations in Central America. Known locally as "baboons," black howler monkeys are an endangered species and are found only in Belize, southern Mexico, and isolated areas of Guatemala. (True baboons live in Africa.) Unlike most wildlife management projects, the Baboon Sanctuary is a voluntary conservation program, supported by private landowners in surrounding villages.

- **Cockscomb Basin Jaguar Preserve:** Below the jagged peaks of the Maya Mountain's Cockscomb Range lies the Cockscomb Basin Jaguar Preserve—an area set aside to help protect endangered jaguars. The preserve also contains many other endangered species, including ocelots, margays, and Baird's tapirs.

For more information about these two preserves, write to:
Belize Audubon Society
Box 1001
Belize City, Belize
Central America

Setting Aside Acres

The Programme for Belize is raising money to pay for and maintain a 110,000-acre tract of tropical forest in Belize. This tract will be managed in cooperation with the government of Belize to save the biological and archaeological treasures of the region. It will also be used for sustainable agricultural research. For information on this program, write to:
Programme for Belize
P.O. Box 385 X
Vineyard Haven, MA 02568

Help for Uganda

Uganda, a small country in central Africa, has lost much of its rain forest to slash-and-burn agriculture and other development projects. To help reforest areas that have been farmed and to help prevent further deforestation, C.A.R.E. is funding several tropical rain forest programs. One

---

helps teach farmers about conserving tropical rain forests. Another is establishing nurseries for raising native species that can be used to reforest areas that have been deforested. For more information, write to:
C.A.R.E.
Donor Services
660 First Ave.
New York, NY 10016

Gorilla-Aid

Mountain gorillas are the most endangered of all the great apes and are considered to be one of the world's most endangered species. Scientists estimate there are fewer than 400 of these creatures left in the wild. In 1979, the African Wildlife Foundation began a conservation program called "The Mountain Gorilla Project" to help protect these vanishing apes. The project helps fund management and education programs in the Parc National des Volcans, Rwanda, Africa—one of the few remaining places where these gorillas are found. To find out more, write to:
African Wildlife Foundation
1717 Massachusetts Ave., NW
Washington, DC 20036

From Borneo to Zaire

Here are two research projects sponsored by Wildlife Conservation International to help protect tropical rain forest species:

- **Okapis Need Help!** Drs. Teresa and John Hart are studying okapis, endangered relatives of giraffes that live in Zaire, Africa. The Harts are working to preserve the habitat where okapis live and to find out more about what these creatures need to survive.

- **The Sarawak Forest Project:** In the Malaysian state of Sarawak, located on the island of Borneo, Elizabeth Bennett

working to preserve rain forest wildlife. With the cooperation of the Sarawak Forest Department, she is surveying different forest types to assess the impact of hunting, logging, slash-and-burn agriculture, and mineral extraction on local wildlife populations.

To find out more about either project, write to:

Wildlife Conservation International
New York Zoological Society
Bronx, NY 10460

Why Save Rain Forests?

Work in teams to discuss reasons for saving tropical rain forests.

Objective:
Describe several reasons why it's important to protect tropical rain forests.

Ages:
Intermediate and advanced

Materials:
copies of page 60
chalkboard or easel
paper
markers

Subjects:
Science and
Social Studies

Malayan flying squirrel

Experts say we're now losing more than 40,000 square miles of tropical rain forests every year—an area about the size of Pennsylvania. And if the present rate continues, there will be almost no tropical rain forests within about 65 years. This gloomy prediction doesn't even take into account increased pressures from growing populations, which could cause the destruction to speed up dramatically.

So what does the loss of thousands of acres of the world's rain forests really mean? In this activity, your group can discuss some of the worldwide consequences of rain forest destruction and why people feel the rain forests of the world need to be protected. Before doing this activity, you may want to do several of the activities in chapters 1, 2, and 3 so that your group has a good feel for what tropical rain forests are and what resources and peoples are found there. Then, after you complete this activity, you might want to see "You Can Help!" on page 52 for some ideas about what your kids can do to help protect tropical rain forests around the world.

DEFORESTATION CONSEQUENCES

First divide the group into teams of four or five children. Have each team come up with a list of reasons why they think the rain forests of the world should be protected. Encourage them to come up with as many reasons as they can. (Also explain that there are many opinions about why we should protect rain forests. However, there are differences of opinion about what's the most important reason to save these tropical treasures.)

After the kids have had about 10 minutes to discuss the question, have each team appoint a spokesperson to report on what each team came up with. As each spokesperson presents the team's ideas, make a master list of reasons on a chalkboard or sheet of easel paper.

Now pass out copies of page 60. Explain that the page contains 10 reasons commonly given for why tropical rain forests should be saved. Ask the team members to compare the master list to the reasons included on the Copycat Page and decide if they want to add anything to the list. You might want to discuss the subtle differences between some of the reasons people give for saving tropical rain forests. For example, some people feel that rain forests should be protected so that native people living in the rain forest are not forced to move and adapt to a new way of life. Other people feel that native people should be protected because they know so much about the plants and animals of the rain forest. According to this reason, native people and their cultural heritage should be protected so that people in developed countries can learn more about rain forest resources that can help the rest of the world.

(continued next page)

After discussing the reasons to save tropical rain forests, have each team get back together and rank the list of reasons in the following ways. (Have each team use the master list you made on the board.) First have the team try to come to some consensus about the two most important reasons to save tropical rain forests. (Each person can pick out one or two reasons and then defend why he or she chose those reasons. Then the team can try to reach a consensus or they can vote on the top two.) Have each team pick a spokesperson to share what the team members came up with and to emphasize the varying views in the group. (The purpose of the ranking is to encourage discussion. Explain to the kids that there is no "most important reason" for saving tropical forests; however, many people feel that some reasons are more urgent than others.)

Next discuss some of the reasons that rain forests are being destroyed. (lumber-

ing tropical forests for valuable har woods, clearing tropical forests for catt ranching, clearing land for cultivatio cutting trees for firewood, harvestir other rain forest products, and so on) U the background information on pag 48–51 to help in your discussion. The ask the kids to look at the master list aga and decide which reasons they thir would best convince other people arour the world—especially those people wl do not know much about rain forests who may not show much interest in hel ing to protect them—that saving tl world's tropical rain forests is importar Are the reasons the same as what the ki individually thought were importan If not, how do they differ?

After your discussion, have each tea prepare an exhibit for the local libra about the effects of tropical rain fore destruction and why it is important to he conserve the world's tropical resources.

Are You Part of the Problem?

Discuss how individual actions can play a part in rain forest problems and solutions.

Objective:
List several problems facing tropical rain forests.

Ages:
Advanced

Materials:
- *copies of discussion questions on page 57*
- *easel paper or chalkboard*

Subjects:
Social Studies and Science

Many of the causes of tropical deforestation don't originate in the tropics at all. Instead, they often originate in developed countries such as the United States, Japan, and many European countries. In this activity, your group can take a look at how individual actions of people in developed countries are having a serious impact on troubled tropical rain forests.

First ask the kids if they can name some of the reasons rain forests are in trouble. List their responses on a chalkboard or sheet of easel paper. Then ask the kids if they think the actions of people in developed countries, such as the United States, contribute to tropical rain forest destruction. If any of the kids think this is true, have them explain how. Then tell them that they'll be learning more about how people in developed countries do affect tropical rain forests.

Now pass out copies of "Are You Pa of the Problem?" on page 57 and have tl kids break up into small groups and di cuss each question as honestly as the can. (You might want to limit the numb of questions they discuss depending c your group's abilities.)

Afterward, discuss how people's a tions in the United States, Europe, Japa Canada, and other developed countri are directly and indirectly affecting tropic rain forest resources. For example, b consuming so many products made fro tropical hardwoods, we are contributir to the depletion of tropical rain forest And by continuing to import tropical bee as many countries are still doing, peop are supporting the cattle ranching indust that destroys thousands of acres of ra forest every year. (Use the backgrour information on pages 48–51 to help wi your discussion.)

1. Some parrots, toucans, and other endangered tropical birds are taken illegally from the tropics and sold in other countries. Some of these birds, however, are raised in captivity and sold legally.
   A. Do you feel that parrots, toucans, or other tropical birds should be kept as pets? Why or why not?
   B. If you saw some of these birds for sale in a pet store, how could you find out if they were taken illegally from another country?
   C. What could you do if you found out that some of the birds were obtained illegally?
   D. What are some ways you could inform other consumers about the problems of smuggling endangered and threatened birds from tropical rain forests?

2. Like many other rain forest plants, many of the valuable hardwoods that grow in tropical rain forests grow far apart from each other. When loggers cut down and remove these hardwoods, such as rosewood and mahogany, they not only deplete the numbers of these trees, they often destroy many other trees in the process. In addition, heavy logging equipment can damage soil and roots. And building logging roads can cause erosion.
   A. Do your parents or friends own furniture made of mahogany, rosewood, or some other tropical tree? If you don't know, how could you find out?
   B. If you knew that something your parents wanted to buy was made from a tropical tree, would you try to convince them not to buy it? If not, why not? If so, how would you convince them?

3. The United States has only about 4 percent of the world's population. Yet we use many times that amount of the world's resources, including wood, energy, food, and medicines. Some of the resources come from the world's tropical rain forests.

yellow-crowned Amazon parrot

   A. What are some ways this enormous use of resources contributes to tropical deforestation?
   B. Can you think of some ways that recycling materials in the United States might help protect rain forest resources in other parts of the world?
   C. What could you do at home or at school to help promote recycling?
   (*Note:* You might want to discuss aluminum as an example of something you use [soft drink cans, aluminum foil, and so on] that has a direct impact on rain forests. In Brazil, for example, rain forests have been flooded to build dams that supply the electricity to process aluminum. Most of the aluminum in these countries is exported to developed countries).

4. If you knew that your favorite type of candy was produced by a company that was supporting projects that destroyed tropical rain forests, would you stop buying it? What do you think is the value of one person boycotting a product? Would you try to get your friends to stop buying the candy? If so, how would you convince them?

5. Would you spend any of your allowance on a project to help protect tropical rain forests? Why or why not? What would make you decide to spend part of your allowance on helping protect tropical rain forests?

6. Read the following quote, which is from a Mayan farmer who lives in southeastern Mexico, and then discuss the questions that follow:

   "The outsiders come into our forest and they cut the mahogany and kill the birds and burn everything. Then they bring in cattle, and the cattle eat the jungle. I think they hate the forest. But I plant my crops and weed them, and I watch the animals, and I watch the forest to know when to plant my corn. As for me, I guard the forest."

   A. Why do you think this farmer resents outsiders?
   B. What do you think the farmer meant when he said "the cattle eat the jungle"?
   C. How do you think the farmer's feelings about the jungle are different from those of the outsiders he is talking about?

7. In 1988, the United States government prohibited the use of the pesticide heptachlor in the U.S. Although it is an effective insecticide, heptachlor was taken off the U.S. market because it is so dangerous to wildlife and people. It can cause cancer and can remain in the environment for decades. The United States still sells heptachlor to other countries, including many countries with tropical rain forests. People use heptachlor to control termites, ants, and other insects.
   A. How do you feel about the United States selling heptachlor to other countries?
   B. Can you think of alternatives to heptachlor, keeping in mind that many people in developing countries are having a difficult time making a living and can't afford higher-priced pesticides?

Issues and Answers

Although tropical rain forests are facing a crisis, many innovative programs and activities—most of them local initiatives—are taking place to help protect these tropical treasures. In this advanced activity, your group can work in teams to take a look at rain forest problems and how local projects and programs are helping to solve some of these problems. And they can present their findings to other group members in an "issues and answers" newscast. (Before starting the activity, you should introduce your group to tropical rain forest basics by having the kids try several activities from chapters 2, and 3.)

PART 1: DEFINING "SUSTAINABLE"

Divide the group into seven teams and give each team a copy of the numbered statements in the margin. Explain that the statements contain information that, together, should help the kids put together a definition for the word "sustainable." Explain that each team should read through the statements, discuss them, and then write their own definition.

Discuss the definitions they come up with, using the definition of sustainable on page 66, and explain how the word "sustainable" applies to problems in rain forests. For example, explain that clearcutting large sections of tropical rain forest for farmland is not a sustainable use of the forest because the land soon becomes depleted of nutrients and crop yields decline until nothing can grow. In other words, rain forest lands can't sustain large-scale agriculture. (See "The Old Ways and the New" on page 35 and "The New Settlers" on page 48 for more information.)

PART 2: SOLUTION SCENARIOS

In this part of the activity, your group will get a chance to investigate some sustainable projects and programs around the world that are helping to protect tropical rain forest resources. First pass out copies of pages 61 and 62 and assign each team one of the problems on page 61. For example, the first team could focus on the loss of rain forest plants and animals (problem 1), and the second team could look at the problems associated with cattle ranching in tropical rain forests (problem 2). Have the team members read through their problems and make sure they understand them. (Use the background information on pages 48–51 to help answer any questions they might have. You might also want to go over some vocabulary words, including definitions for "indigenous" and "slash-and-burn agriculture." See the glossary on page 66.)

Then have the kids look at the section titled "What's Working." Explain that these are descriptions of projects or programs in different parts of the world that are helping people that live in these areas make a living without permanently damaging the natural resources the people depend on. As the kids read through the descriptions, encourage them to look up words they don't know, such as "exploitation" and "perennial." (With less advanced students, you might want to spend some time discussing the solutions as a group before going on.)

Explain that each team should discuss the problem they have been given and think about how the projects and programs working in other parts of the world might apply to their problem. Encourage them to think about how similar solutions could help solve their problem. For example, some people are trying to protect plant and animal species in tropical rain forests by setting aside large tracts of forest for parks. Other people are conducting research on what specific plants and animals need to survive. And in some parts of the world, education programs in schools and communities are also helping.

Also have each team brainstorm other solutions that might help solve the problem. Have team members look at the pros and cons of each "solution" they came up with and generate a list of as many ideas as they can that might help solve the problem they were assigned.

After the teams have had time to discuss their problems and generate a list of solutions, tell each group to prepare a short "newscast" for an "issues and answers" news program so that everyone can learn more about rain forest problems and solutions. Each team can present their problems in a creative way, along with some of the solutions they came up with. After each team's presentation, discuss the problems and solutions with the rest of the group. (See "Discussing Problems and Solutions" below to help with the discussion.)

After all the teams have made their presentations, emphasize again that many people around the world—those that live in tropical rain forests and those that don't—are trying to protect these important habitats. And even though there are many problems facing rain forests, there are many things that people can do to help. (See "You Can Help!" on page 52 for more about what you can do.)

Much of the information in this activity was adapted with permission from *Saving the Tropical Forests* by Judith Gradwohl and Russell Greenberg (Earthscan Publications LTD and Island Press, 1988.)

DISCUSSING PROBLEMS AND SOLUTIONS

Problem 1: Many tropical rain forest plants and animals are becoming extinct.
- setting aside rain forest land for parks can help protect endangered species
- research can help determine how to best protect plant and animal species
- raising animals in captivity for food and other products can help protect wild populations

Problem 2: Cattle ranching causes deforestation and soil erosion.
- dairy farming can be less harmful to rain forests than beef farming if the dairy cattle are raised in enclosures; dairy cattle can provide meat *and* milk products
- raising native animals in captivity can help protect wild animal populations and provide food for people

Problem 3: Large-scale, single-crop farming is often not sustainable and is prone to pests and disease.
- mixed plantings are usually more sustainable than single-crop farming
- research is helping develop sustainable methods that produce more food on smaller areas of land
- small-plot farming is often more sustainable than large-scale farming

Problem 4: Too many people are moving into rain forests and cutting and burning the forests to raise crops. This "slash-and-burn" agriculture is not sustainable when too many people practice it in a small area.
- using the knowledge indigenous peoples have about rain forests can help develop sustainable agriculture projects
- relying on a mix of sustainable agriculture and other development projects, such as properly managed tourism, small garden plots, sustainable timber harvesting, and so on, can help protect forest resources
- planting trees can help regenerate forests and provide food and fuelwood
- extractive reserves allow people to make a living in the forest without destroying it

Problem 5: Many tropical countries owe huge sums of money to foreign banks and are relying on short-term exploitation of their rain forests (such as the sale of exotic timber to developed nations) to help pay off these debts.
- debt-for-nature swaps can help ease a country's national debt and protect forest resources at the same time

- properly managed tourism and sustainable timbering operations and agriculture projects can help bring money into a country and protect natural resources

Problem 6: Deforestation is harming indigenous peoples throughout the tropics.
- getting the support and advice of indigenous peoples can help ensure the success of a tropical rain forest reserve
- using the knowledge indigenous peoples have about rain forests can help develop sustainable agriculture projects

Problem 7: Deforestation causes soil erosion.
- well-managed garden plots help families grow the food they need and can help prevent soil erosion
- low-impact tree harvesting helps protect forest soil
- limiting cattle ranching and slash-and-burn agriculture on steep slopes helps control tropical deforestation and soil erosion

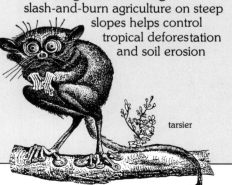

tarsier

59

TEN REASONS TO SAVE TROPICAL RAIN FORESTS

1 Many scientists think that destroying tropical rain forests could drastically change world weather patterns.

2 Tropical rain forests contain more than 50 percent of all plant and animal species in the world. If the rain forests are destroyed, most of these plant and animal species will be lost forever. Scientists predict this loss of species diversity would have serious consequences for the health of the planet.

3 Scientists have studied only a small percentage of the plants and animals that live in tropical rain forests. Every day we are losing species that could potentially provide people with new products and medicines, such as gasoline substitutes and cancer cures.

4 Tropical rain forests are exotic and unique wild places where amazing and strange plants and animals live. They have long inspired artists, scientists and others. Loss of these incredibly diverse forests would be a serious loss for everyone.

5 As rain forests disappear, so will the cultural traditions of many native peoples. These indigenous peoples have a right to live where and how they want.

6 As native rain forest peoples die or are forced to move, the world will lose their knowledge of rain forest plants, animals and other information that took indigenous peoples hundreds of years to gather. This information about what's in the rain forest and how it "works" could help scientists develop new crops, medicines and other products.

7 Many species around the world, including many North American songbirds that migrate to Latin America, depend on the tropics for survival. As more and more rain forest habitats disappear, the loss will affect many of the migrating species

8 People who live outside of tropical rain forests depend on products from rain forests, including valuable hardwoods such as mahogany; and foods such as bananas, nuts and coffee. As the destruction continues, these products could become very scarce and more expensive.

9 The loss of thousands of acres of tropical rain forests is already causing serious local problems, including increased soil erosion and water pollution. As more deforestation occurs, the problems will increase.

10 People don't have the right to destroy the world's rain forests and other habitats for their own purposes.

PROBLEMS

1 Scientists estimate that we are losing more than 40,000 square miles of tropical rain forest each year. This deforestation is wiping out tropical species that we don't even know exist.

2 In many areas—especially in Central and South America—cattle ranching for beef production has destroyed millions of acres of tropical rain forest. Unfortunately, most of the beef and profits do not go to the poor people who need them most. Cattle ranching also causes serious erosion problems, and eventually wears out the land.

3 In many parts of the tropics, the most fertile land is often owned by large companies who invest in large-scale, commercial farms. Most of these farms cultivate only a few major crops, and sell what they grow to other countries. By relying on only a few crops, these farms are often more prone to pest and disease problems than smaller, mixed-crop farms.

4 In many countries, slash-and-burn agriculture is a leading cause of tropical deforestation. Slash-and-burn agriculture is a farming method in which patches of rain forest are cut and then burned to clear the land for crops. During the first few years, the crops do well, nourished by the nutrients that were in the ash and soil. But if the land is not allowed to "rest" after it's been cultivated for a while, the soil becomes worn out and the plot is abandoned or taken over by cattle ranchers.

On a small scale, slash-and-burn agriculture can be sustainable—but only if land that has been cleared is allowed to remain fallow for many years, giving the forest and soil time to regenerate. Unfortunately, in many areas too many people and not enough resources mean that land does not have a chance to recover.

5 Many developing tropical countries owe huge sums of money to banks in the United States and other developed countries. To repay the money they borrowed, many of these tropical countries rely on non-sustainable uses of rain forest, such as cattle ranching and poorly managed timber harvesting.

6 Tropical deforestation is having a direct impact on indigenous tribes who live in rain forests. In many cases, indigenous people are forced to move or are relocated through government programs. Indigenous people have also suffered from diseases brought by settlers and other "outsiders."

7 Tropical deforestation creates serious soil erosion problems in many tropical areas. Trees help hold soil in place and keep it from washing away. The soil that washes away from once-forested land runs into streams and rivers, blocking transportation routes and sometimes killing fish and other wildlife.

WHAT'S WORKING

1 By visiting parks and reserves in tropical rain forests, bird watchers and other nature enthusiasts from developed countries bring needed money into developing countries. Since these tourists help support local economies (by staying in hotels, eating at restaurants, buying local crafts, and so on), native people are often encouraged to protect natural areas and establish nature centers, trails, and facilities to help encourage tourists to visit.

2 In Java, home gardens known as *pekarangan* are one of the most important sources of food on the island. Home gardens mimic the structure of the real forest and contain a variety of plants, from ground-growing vines to tall trees. For example, vegetables such as spinach and beans, along with medicinal plants, grow on the ground. Taller plants, such as banana and papaya, grow above these vegetables and medicinal plants. Small trees, including citrus, guava, coffee, and cacao, make up an even higher level. And the tallest layers include jackfruit, mango, bamboo, and sugar palm. Among other things, this "layered approach" helps reduce soil erosion by breaking the pounding of the rain.

3 In 1985, the Community Baboon Sanctuary was established in Belize to protect one of the few remaining black howler monkey populations in Central America. Unlike most wildlife management projects, the sanctuary depends on the cooperation of private landowners. Nearly all of

ISSUES AND ANSWERS

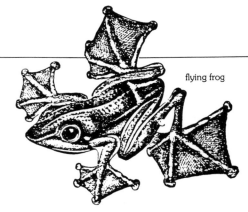
flying frog

them have agreed to follow a conservation plan to enhance and protect the howlers' habitat. The plan includes protecting forests along riverbanks and leaving food trees standing when clearing land. Through sustainable land use practices and voluntary cooperation, these landowners are helping to protect the black howler monkey and its habitat in Belize.

4 For nearly 30 years, the Corporation Carton de Colombia in South America has been practicing sustainable harvesting of trees in tropical rain forests. The logging causes little damage to the soil because trees are cut carefully and the logs are removed with aerial cables, instead of heavy logging equipment. And only certain areas are allowed to be logged at any one time. In addition, this commercial operation has supported research to learn more about how rain forests can regenerate and has replanted areas that have been clearcut.

5 In many areas, government officials and conservationists are encouraging cattle ranchers to become dairy farmers. Although any kind of cattle project has negative effects on the rain forest, dairy farming can be less harmful to the environment because the cattle are contained in pens and damage a smaller area than beef cattle. Dairy cattle can also provide year-round income. Beef cattle go to market only once or twice a year, but farmers that raise dairy cattle can always sell milk and other dairy products.

6 Farmers in Iquitos, Peru cultivate annual crops, such as manioc, rice, and plantain, with perennial crops, such as fruit and nut trees. While the fruit and nut trees are maturing, the annual crops produce food. Several plots are farmed at the same time, and some plots are allowed to lie fallow so nutrients can rebuild in the soil. Farming practices like these require less weeding and care than other types of farming practices.

7 In Panama and Costa Rica, raising iguanas in captivity provides a source of protein for people, and at the same time protects wild iguanas. People in Central America have always relied on iguanas as a source of meat and eggs. But overharvesting has reduced their numbers in the wild substantially. The iguana ranching project releases captive-reared iguanas in forested areas. Many people feel that iguana ranching makes better economic sense than cattle ranching. And it does much less harm to the environment.

8 In 1985, Ecuador established a tree-planting fund called "Plan Bosque." This fund provides loans to people and community groups to plant and care for trees in areas where wood shortages are critical. If the trees are well-taken care of and healthy two years into the project, Plan Bosque will pay off the loan. If the trees are not cared for, then the borrower must pay off the loan.

9 For hundreds of years, the Kayapo Indians of the eastern Amazon Basin of Brazil have been using a complex system of tropical forest management. They complete an ecological inventory of a site, identifying plants and soil types before deciding what to do with an area. They also practice controlled slash-and-burn agriculture. The Kayapo continually mulch the soil to add nutrients and they manage fallow land for wildlife habitat. Scientists think this sustainable system could have great applications in other parts of the world.

10 Since 1987, several debt-for-nature deals have been successfully carried out. By working with banks, conservation groups have been able to lower tropical country debt payments in exchange for the country agreeing to protect tropical rain forests.

11 For years, people in Brazil's rain forests have been tapping rubber trees for latex, collecting Brazil nuts, and harvesting other natural products in a way that doesn't destroy the forest. In the past few years, many of these rubber tappers have joined together and pressured the government into setting up special reserves that allow them to continue this sustainable way of life. These *extractive reserves* provide an on-going source of income for rain forest residents. Conservationists hope that extractive reserves will be set up in other parts of Brazil and South America.

ake a life-sized
orpho butterfly to
ear on your finger.

es:
imary and
termediate

aterials:
copies of the pattern
below
crayons or colored
pencils
scissors
pushpins
black pipe cleaners
rulers
pictures of morpho
butterflies (optional)

bjects:
ts and Crafts

In the rain forests of Central and South America huge, shiny blue butterflies called morphos gracefully flutter, as though in slow motion, through the dim forest understory. Your kids can make their own life-sized morphos by following these directions. (You may want to show the kids pictures of morphos first.)

1. Color the morpho pattern bright blue and then cut it out.
2. Color the undersides of the wings brown and the underside of the body black.
3. Fold the butterfly in half along the body. Match the wings together and crease on the underside.
4. Unfold the butterfly. Using a pushpin, poke a hole through each of the two white circles on the butterfly's body.
5. Cut a 4-inch piece of black pipe cleaner and fold it into a U-shape. (There should be an equal amount of pipe cleaner on either side of the U.)
6. Starting from the morpho's underside, poke each end of the pipe cleaner U through one of the holes in the body until about an inch of each end is visible from the morpho's upper side.
7. Slip your index finger through the pipe cleaner loop poking out of the butterfly's underside. Make the ring fairly snug (but not too tight) by gently pushing the morpho closer to your finger and then twisting the pipe cleaner together on the morpho's upper side. (Be sure to twist only once!)
8. Bend the excess pipe cleaner up between the morpho's wings to form antennae (see photo).
9. Hold out your index finger and make a fist with your other fingers and your thumb. Then gently move your hand up and down and watch your butterfly flutter!

se Woelflein

Beautiful Bromeliads

Make a paper bromeliad.

Ages:
Primary and Intermediate

Materials:
- *copies of the patterns on page 65*
- *pictures of bromeliads*
- *toilet paper rolls (one per person)*
- *green and blue construction paper*
- *pencils*
- *scissors*
- *clear tape*
- *crayons or markers*
- *glue (optional)*

Subjects:
Arts and Crafts

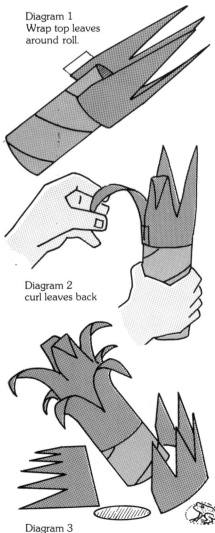

Diagram 1
Wrap top leaves around roll.

Diagram 2
curl leaves back

Diagram 3
position second set of leaves so that it falls between first set

Tropical rain forests are often full of bromeliads (bro-MEAL-ee-ads)—plants that grow on the trunks and branches of trees. Some of the bigger bromeliads are lush, leafy, mini-habitats that make perfect high-rise homes for frogs, insects, snakes, and other animals.

Your kids can make their own bromeliads out of construction paper and toilet paper rolls. But before they start, show them some pictures of bromeliads. Then pass out copies of the patterns on the next page and have the kids follow these instructions:

1. Cut out the pattern marked "top leaves." Trace around the pattern onto green construction paper, then cut out the traced pattern.
2. Cut out the pattern marked "bottom leaves." Trace around the pattern onto green construction paper *three times*, then cut out all three traced patterns. Put these patterns aside for now.
3. Wrap the first leaf pattern you cut out (from step 1) around the top of the toilet paper roll so that most of the construction paper extends beyond the end of the roll (see diagram 1).
4. Tape the two ends of the construction paper together, and then tape the construction paper to the toilet paper roll.

Diagram 4
tape or glue frog to a leaf

5. Curl back each leaf by curling around your fingers and holding it place for a few seconds (see diagra 2).
6. Wrap one of the leaf patterns fro step 2 around the toilet paper r so that it overlaps the bottom the first set of leaves. Tape the tu ends of this set of leaves toget er—but before you tape it in pla on the toilet paper roll, shift around so that each leaf will fa more or less between two "top leaves (see diagram 3). Then ct the leaves as you did in step 5.
7. Wrap the remaining two leaf patter around the toilet paper roll one at time, making sure each leaf falls b tween leaves already taped in plac Curl the leaves. (The last leaf patte should cover the rest of the toi paper roll. Trim any excess constru tion paper that's protruding from t bottom of the roll.)
8. Cut out the pattern marked "w ter." Trace around the pattern on blue piece of construction pap and cut it out. Gently push it in the top of the bromeliad till it f snugly onto the top of the toil paper roll. (*Note:* To fit well, tl water pattern should be slight wider than the toilet paper roll. the pattern we've provided isr the right size, make your own circ of water by tracing around you toilet paper roll. Be sure to trace : that the circle is slightly larg around than the roll.)
9. Color the frog pattern and cut it ou (Some tropical frogs are bright red oranges, blues, greens, and oth colors.)
10. Tape or glue the frog to a bromelia leaf (see diagram 4).
11. If you want, you can color the tips your bromeliad leaves. Some br meliad leaf tips are red, orange, pink.

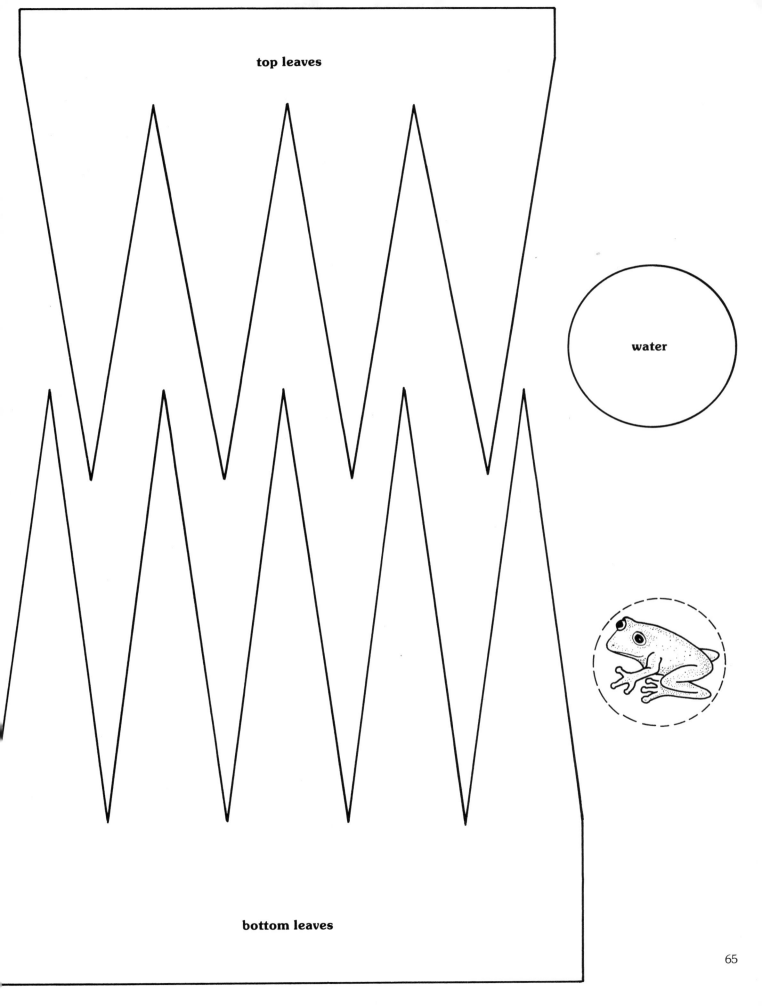

top leaves

water

bottom leaves

APPENDIX

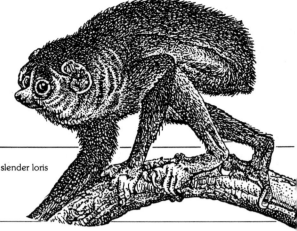

slender loris

Glossary

bromeliads—tropical plants in the pineapple family that often grow on the trunks and branches of trees.

buttresses—woody flanges that radiate from the bases of some tall tropical forest trees. Many scientists think buttresses help support shallow-rooted trees, which might otherwise blow down easily.

canopy—the layer of a forest formed by the crowns of tall trees. In a tropical rain forest, the canopy is made up of flat-crowned trees that are often about 65–100 feet tall.

deforestation—the destruction of a forest. In the tropics, deforestation is caused by a number of activities, such as slash-and-burn agriculture, cattle ranching, and timber harvesting.

emergent—a tree that grows taller than the canopy trees around it. Emergents have umbrella-shaped crowns and slender trunks, and they may grow to be more than 200 feet tall.

epiphyte—a plant that grows on other plants. The roots of many epiphytes can absorb moisture directly from the air.

ethnobotany—the study of how people use plants.

hunter-gatherers—people who get most or all of the food they need by hunting and by gathering wild plants.

indigenous—occurring naturally in a certain area. "Indigenous people" is most often used to mean the tribal peoples, such as American Indians, who lived in an area before Europeans arrived.

jungle—a general term used to describe tropical forests, and often used interchangeably with the term "tropical rain forest." "Jungle" can be misleading because it's often used to describe areas of impenetrable vegetation. But rain forests and many other tropical forests typically don't have a thick layer of undergrowth, except at their edges.

liana—a woody vine that is rooted in the soil and grows up tree trunks or in open areas.

shaman—a tribal priest and/or doctor who often has great knowledge of the medicinal qualities of native plants.

slash-and-burn agriculture—the method of agriculture in which people clear land by cutting down patches of forest and burning the debris. When too many people practice slash-and-burn agriculture in an area and don't allow enough time for the cleared land to lie fallow before cultivating it again, the area can become permanently damaged.

sustainable development—development that uses natural resources in an efficient way and without destroying the basis of their productivity. Sustainable development allows natural resources to regenerate. Many indigenous people have practiced sustainable slash-and-burn agriculture in tropical forests for hundreds of years.

tropical rain forest—an evergreen forest located at low elevations in regions between the Tropics of Cancer and Capricorn. Tropical rain forests are characterized by abundant rainfall and a very warm, humid climate year-round. Other types of tropical forests include *cloud forests*, which occur at high elevations, and *seasonal forests*, which have wet and dry seasons.

understory—the forest layer beneath the canopy that includes small trees, young canopy trees, shrubs, and herbs.

Note: A ◀ at the end of a listing indicates that the book is a good source of rain forest pictures.

GENERAL REFERENCE BOOKS

Dreams of Amazonia by Roger D. Stone (Viking, 1985)
The Enchanted Canopy by Andrew W. Mitchell (Macmillan, 1986)
In the Rainforest by Catherine Caufield (Knopf, 1985)
The International Book of the Forest (Simon & Schuster, 1981) ◀
Life Above the Jungle Floor by Donald Perry (Simon & Schuster, 1986)
The Life and Mysteries of the Jungle edited by Edward S. Ayensu (Crescent, 1980) ◀
The Life of the Jungle by Paul W. Richards (McGraw-Hill, 1970) ◀
People of the Tropical Rain Forest edited by Julie Sloan Denslow and Christine Padoch (University of California Press, 1988) ◀
The Primary Source: Tropical Forests and Our Future by Norman Myers (Norton, 1984)
Rain Forests and Cloud Forests by Michael Emsley (Abrams, 1979) ◀
Saving the Tropical Forests by Judith Gradwohl and Russell Greenberg (Earthscan, 1988; paperback edition distributed in the U.S. by Agribookstore, 1611 N. Kent St., Arlington, VA 22209)
Tropical Nature by Andrew Forsyth and Kenneth Miyata (Charles Scribner's Sons, 1984)
Tropical Rainforest by Arnold Newman (Facts on File, 1990) ◀

CHILDREN'S BOOKS

Animals in Danger: Forests of Africa compiled by Gill Gould (Rourke, 1982). Advanced
Animals of the Tropical Forests by Sylvia A. Johnson (Lerner, 1976). Intermediate ◀
A Closer Look at Jungles by Joyce Pope (Gloucester, 1978). Intermediate and Advanced
Disappearing Rainforest by Robert Prosser (Dryad, 1987). Advanced
The Great Kapok by Lynne Cherry (Gulliver, 1990). Intermediate
Journey Through a Tropical Jungle by Adrian Forsyth (Simon & Schuster, 1988). Intermediate and Advanced ◀
The Jungle by Carroll R. Norden (Raintree, 1988). Primary and Intermediate
Jungles by Andrew Langley (Bookwright, 1987). Intermediate and Advanced ◀
Jungles by Illa Podendorf (Childrens Press, 1982). Primary and Intermediate ◀
Jungles by Angela Wilkes (EDC, 1980). Primary and Intermediate
The Jungles: A Science Activity Book (Puffin, 1987). All Ages ◀
Nature Hide & Seek: Jungles by John Norris Wood and Kevin Dean (Knopf, 1987). All Ages ◀
Rain Forest Homes by Althea (Cambridge University Press, 1985). Primary
The Rainforest Children by Margaret Pittaway (Oxford, 1980). Primary
Rainforest Secrets by Arthur Dorros (Scholastic, 1990). Intermediate and Advanced ◀
The Tropical Forest by Mary Batten (Crowell, 1973). Advanced
Where the Forest Meets the Sea by Jeannie Baker (Greenwillow, 1987). Primary and Intermediate

Wonders of the Jungle edited by Victor H. Waldrop (National Wildlife Federation, 1986). Intermediate and Advanced ◀
Wonders of the Rain Forest by Janet Craig (Troll, 1990)

CASSETTES, FILMS, FILMSTRIPS, SLIDES, AND VIDEOS

Biomes: Tropical Rainforest (Advanced) is available from Coronet Film and Video, 420 Academy Dr., Northbrook, IL 60062.
Disappearance of the Great Rain Forest (Advanced) is available in film or video from Arthur Mokin Productions, Inc., P.O. Box 1866, Santa Rosa, CA 95402.
Jungles: The Green Oceans (Advanced) is available in film or video from Encyclopaedia Britannica, and highlights predator/prey relationships and adaptations of wildlife in jungles. Order from Encyclopaedia Britannica Educational Corp., 310 S. Michigan Ave., Chicago, IL 60604.
Rain Forest (Advanced) is available in video or film from National Geographic Society, Educational Services, Dept. 91, Washington, DC 20036.
The Rain Forest (Advanced) is a slide set available from Carolina Biological Supply Co., 2700 York Rd., Burlington, NC 27215. Describes rain forests along the Napo River in Ecuador, concentrating on plants and their use by natives.
Rain Forest Rap (Intermediate and Advanced), produced by the World Wildlife Fund, is a six-minute video set to rap music. It shows the problems facing tropical rain forests and how kids can help. It is available from Publications Dept. OB, World Wildlife Fund, P.O. Box 4866, Hampden Station, Baltimore, MD 21211. (This video can also be ordered as part of a teacher's kit. See "Other Activity Sources" on page 68.)
The Tropical Rain Forest Set (All Ages) contains slides and a booklet with background information. *Tropical Rain Forests Under Fire* (Intermediate and Advanced) is a filmstrip with activity booklet and narrative cassette. Both are available from Educational Images Ltd., P.O. Box 3456, West Side, Elmira, NY 14905.
Voices of the Peruvian Rain Forest is a cassette available from Cornell University Laboratory of Ornithology, 159 Sapsucker Woods Rd., Ithaca, NY 14850.
Why Are the Forests Disappearing? (Intermediate and Advanced) is a video available from Agency for Instructional Technology, Box A, Bloomington, IN 47402.
Wildlife in the Jungles of Latin America (Intermediate) is a film available from International Film Bureau, Inc., 332 S. Michigan Ave., Chicago, IL 60604.

BOOKLETS, PERIODICALS, AND POSTERS

The Canopy is published quarterly by the Rainforest Alliance and contains background information, current topics and events, and a list of resources on tropical forests. For subscription information write Rainforest Alliance, 270 Lafayette, Suite 512, New York, NY, 10012.
Center for Marine Conservation has an informative handout on how the destruction of rain forests affects life in neighboring coral reef communities. To order a copy, write Center for Marine Conservation, 1725 DeSales St., NW, Suite 500, Washington, DC 20036.
Rainforest Action Network offers a "Save the Rainforest" poster. For more information write Rainforest Action Network, 301 Broadway, Suite A, San Francisco, CA 94133.

Other Activity Sources

Marine World Africa USA has a teacher's guide with activities about rain forests for grades K-12. Included are worksheets, puzzles, flashcards, and conservation tips. Send your request to Marine World Africa USA, Marine World Foundation, Marine World Pkwy., Vallejo, CA 94589.

National Audubon Society has a poster on tropical forests along with a teacher's guide suggesting activities to use with the poster (Intermediate and Advanced). An information booklet, "Who's Killing the Forests?" is also available. Write to National Audubon Society, 801 Pennsylvania Ave., SE, Washington, DC 20003.

Vanishing Rain Forests (All Ages) is an educational packet produced by the World Wildlife Fund to accompany the Smithsonian Institution's traveling exhibit, "Tropical Rainforests: A Disappearing Treasure." The packet contains a video, full-color poster, background information, and teacher's guide with rain forest activities. For more information, write Publications Department OB, World Wildlife Fund, P.O. Box 4866, Hampden Station, Baltimore, MD 21211.

Where To Get More Information

- college and university departments of natural resources, biology, botany, and zoology
- organizations working to protect tropical rain forests (for a partial list, see page 54)
- zoos, museums, and botanical gardens with rain forest exhibits (see list on next page)

Ranger Rick Tropical Rain Forest Index

Ranger Rick, *published by the National Wildlife Federation, is a monthly nature magazine for elementary-age children.*

Where to See Tropical Rain Forests

There may be a "rain forest" closer than you think! Below is a list of zoological parks and other institutions that have tropical rain forest exhibits or educational programs. Be sure to call before you visit to find out what exhibits or programs are suitable for your group. Also check to see if you need to make any special arrangements for a group visit.

Binder Park Zoo, 7400 Division Dr., Battle Creek, MI 49017 **

Birmingham Zoo, c/o Alabama Zoological Society, Box 74022, Birmingham, AL 35253

Brandywine Zoo, 1001 N. Park Dr., Wilmington, DE 19802

Buffalo Zoological Gardens, Delaware Park, Buffalo, NY 14214

Burnet Park Zoo, Box 146, Liverpool, NY 13088

Calgary Zoo, Box 3036, Station "B," Calgary, Alberta, Canada T2M 4R8

Chicago Zoological Park (Brookfield Zoo), 3300 Golf Rd., Brookfield, IL 60513

Cleveland Metroparks Zoo, 3900 Brookside Park Dr., Cleveland, OH 44109

Cincinnati Zoo, 3400 Vine St., Cincinnati, OH 45220

Denver Zoological Gardens, City Park, Denver, CO 80205

Discovery Place, 301 N. Tryon St., Charlotte, NC 28202

The Fresno Zoo, 894 W. Belmont Ave., Fresno, CA 93728

Henry Vilas Zoo, 702 S. Randall Ave., Madison, WI 53715

Hogle Zoological Garden, Box 8475, Salt Lake City, UT 84108

Indianapolis Zoo, 1200 W. Washington St., Indianapolis, IN 46222-4552

Jackson Zoological Park, 2918 W. Capitol St., Jackson, MS 39209

John G. Shedd Aquarium, 1200 S. Lake Shore Dr., Chicago, IL 60605

Kansas City Zoological Gardens, Swope Park, Kansas City, MO 64132

Little Rock Zoological Gardens, #1 Jonesboro Dr., Little Rock, AR 72205

Los Angeles Zoo, 5333 Zoo Dr., Los Angeles, CA 90027

Louisville Zoological Garden, 1100 Trevilian Way, P.O. Box 37250, Louisville, KY 40233

Marine World Africa, Marine World Pkwy., Vallejo, CA 94589

Mesker Park Zoo, Bement Ave., Evansville, IN 47712

Metropolitan Toronto Zoo, Box 280, West Hill, Toronto, Ontario, Canada, MIE 4RS

Miller Park Zoo, Box 3157, Bloomington, IL 61702

Milwaukee Public Museum, 800 W. Wells St., Milwaukee, WI 53233

Minnesota Zoological Garden, 12101 Johnny Cake Ridge Rd., Apple Valley, MN 55124

Monkey Jungle, Box 246, Miami, FL 33170

National Aquarium in Baltimore, Pier 3, 501 E. Pratt St., Baltimore, MD 21202

New England Aquarium, Central Wharf, Boston, MA 02110

New York Zoological Park (Bronx Zoo), 185th St. and Southern Blvd., Bronx, NY 10460

North Carolina Zoological Park, Rt. 4, Box 83, Asheboro, NC 27203

Philadelphia Zoological Garden, 34th St. and Girard Ave., Philadelphia, PA 19104

Pittsburgh Aviary, Allegheny Commons West, Pittsburgh, PA 15212 **

Reid Park Zoo, 900 S. Randolph Way, Tucson, AZ 85716 **

Riverbanks Zoological Park, 500 Wildlife Pkwy., Columbia, SC 29210

San Diego Zoo, Box 551, San Diego, CA 92112

Santa Ana Zoo, 1801 E. Chestnut Ave., Santa Ana, CA 92701 **

Santa Barbara Zoological Gardens, 500 Ninos Dr., Santa Barbara, CA 93103

Sedgwick County Zoo and Botanical Garden, 5555 Zoo Blvd., Wichita, KS 67212

Staten Island Zoo, 614 Broadway, Staten Island, NY 10310 *

Toledo Zoological Gardens, 2700 Broadway, Toledo, OH 43609

Topeka Zoological Park, 635 Gage Blvd., Topeka, KS 66606

Vancouver Public Aquarium, Box 3232, Vancouver, British Columbia, Canada V6B 3X8

Zoo Atlanta, 800 Cherokee Ave., SE, Atlanta, GA 30315

* indicates this exhibit is under development, to be completed by end of 1991
** no separate exhibit, but offers programs on rain forests

leopard cat

1997 UPDATE

TABLE OF CONTENTS

ailed macaque

71

WHAT'S HAPPENING WITH RAIN FORESTS?

Carolyn Duckworth

C hildren who read *Ranger Rick®* magazine often learn about rain forests and the amazing animals that inhabit them. They also learn how rain forests are being harmed by the activities of some people and helped by the activities of others. Some of the articles include a story about the Children's Rainforest in Monte Verde, Costa Rica; the threats to Hawaii's rain forests; and the role rain forests play in the lives of migratory songbirds. (You'll find a list in the back of this book.)

The rain forests are still threatened, but the good news is that there are many people and programs helping to protect these vital ecosystems. The Rainforest Alliance is one of the most active groups working to help rain forests. If you would like to join this effort, there are several Rainforest Alliance programs that make interesting and rewarding class projects.

The Banana Project

Bananas are America's favorite fruit, but the practices used to grow bananas have been threatening rain forests for many years. (See *Ranger Rick®* magazine, February 1994.) Banana farmers cut down rain forests to make room to grow bananas. They use strong chemicals to make the fruit grow faster, and those chemicals pollute rivers and soil. Banana growers put plastic bags over bananas to protect them from insects and help them ripen. When they finish using the bags, the growers throw the plastic on the ground. The bags often wash into rivers and the ocean, where they can injure animals that live there.

blue-and-yellow
macaw

The Banana Project, part of the Rainforest Alliance's "Eco O.K." program, asks children and other people who love bananas to write to the big banana companies and ask them to make their farms "Eco-O.K." Chiquita Brands is one of the biggest banana companies. It has responded to these letters by certifying most of its farms. In order to be certified, banana growers must agree to:

- Plant tropical rain forest trees and plants along the rivers and roads around their banana plantations.

- Offer environmental education to the people who live and work on the farms.

- Recycle the plastic bags they use to protect banana plants.

- Reduce their use of chemicals.

This project is still active. You can help by writing to the banana companies and asking them to certify their farms. Here are the addresses of some of the companies:

Abelareo Sanchez
Chief Executive Officer
Del Monte Fresh Produce Company
800 Douglas Entrance, North Tower
Coral Gables, FL 33134
U.S.A.

David Murdock
Chief Executive Officer
Dole Food Company
31355 Oak Crest Drive
Westlake Village, CA 91361
U.S.A.

If you write to Chiquita, be sure to thank them for joining this important project.

Carl Lindner
Chief Operating Officer
Chiquita Brands
250 East 5th Street
Cincinnati, OH 45202
U.S.A.

Smart Wood Program

Many musical instruments are made from rain forest wood. The good news is that the Gibson company is now making guitars that are "rain-forest friendly." These guitars look as beautiful and sound as good as other guitars, but they are made with wood that is harvested in an environmentally healthy way.

Gibson USA participates in the Rainforest Alliance's "Smart Wood" program. In operation since 1990, this program certifies companies that process and sell wood products made of wood that was harvested in an environmentally responsible way. Smart Wood certification requires that companies protect the local environment and water, minimize damage to remaining forests, prevent overcutting of forests, and develop good relations with local communities. You can find out about other companies that participate in the Smart Wood program by writing to the Rainforest Alliance or visiting its site on the World Wide Web. (You'll find the address below.)

Allies in the Rainforests

jaguar

The Rainforest Alliance publishes *Allies in the Rainforest*, a guide to projects dedicated to protecting the world's rain forests and the animals that live there. These projects include:

- Buying rain forest land in El Salvador and Costa Rica;

- Working with Mayan Indians to protect migratory songbirds;

- Working with people in Madagascar who are trying to save the lemurs.

Kids individually and in groups can donate to these projects. Schools often hold rain forest education programs or walkathons to raise money. Donations of any size are welcomed and will be sent to the project you choose from the *Allies in the Rainforest* catalog.

Rain Forests on the World Wide Web

Check out the Rainforest Alliance's site on the World Wide Web. It provides a clearinghouse for rain forest and conservation education, course materials to download, rain forest reading and movie lists, classroom activities, discussion groups, and bulletin boards. Visitors to this site can also see pictures of wildlife and plants that live in the rain forest. The address is

http://www.rainforest-alliance.org

Many other groups work to protect rain forests. You might want to contact the Rainforest Action Network (known as "RAN"). RAN reports that kids around the world have donated thousands of dollars to its program, "Protect an Acre." RAN also sponsors an art contest for elementary students around the world. To find out more, look at the RAN homepage on the World Wide Web. The address is

http://www.ran.org

LONG DISTANCE TRAVELERS

Carolyn Duckworth

Each year people in North America play host to millions of visitors from the tropics. But these visitors aren't people; they're birds! Many species of hummingbirds, swallows, warblers, flycatchers, hawks, and sparrows spend most of the year in the tropical rain forests, tropical dry forests, and grasslands of Central America, South America, and the islands of the Caribbean Sea. In spring, these birds fly thousands of miles north to reach the forests, grasslands, wetlands, and tundra of North America. There they nest and raise their young before flying south again in the fall.

Colorful Signs of Spring

Birds that make this yearly journey from the tropics to North America are called *neotropical migrants*. For many people, neotropical migrants are an important, personal connection between their daily lives and the tropical rain forests far away. Each spring, they look forward to seeing the bright orange feathers of northern orioles, the deep reds of scarlet tanagers, and the flashing, jewel-like colors of ruby-throated humming-birds. These people rejoice when they hear the watery, melodious songs of wood thrushes and veeries. They have the pleasure of seeing warblers build nests and raise their young. Often they think of these visitors as "their birds," but really, these birds spend much more time in Central and South America than they spend in North America. Neotropical migrants are something that the people of North, South, and Central America share every year.

Incredible Journeys

All birds of the same species look pretty much alike, but scientists have a way of telling one bird from another. They put small, plastic, color-coded bracelets called bands on the legs of some birds. The bands identify individual birds. Through banding, scientists have been able to prove that an individual bird may fly thousands of miles south to the tropical rain forest, yet fly all the way back the next year to nest in the very same tree it nested in the year before. So it is possible that you might recognize some of "your birds" from their visit last year.

Migration, however, is dangerous. Almost half of the migrating birds that leave North America in the fall do not return in the spring. They die during the long journey south or north, or during their stay in the tropics. Many of these deaths are natural. Bird populations can recover from these losses, and have, year after year. But in the last few decades, bird watchers have seen a drastic decline in the populations of many neotropical migrants. Where once there were huge flocks of many, many birds, now there might be only a small number of birds scattered here and there. Bird watchers today have to search longer and harder to find bird species that were once relatively easy to find.

Dangerous Declines

Scientific studies prove what bird watchers suspect is true—that many bird populations are declining. Each year two thousand volunteers in North America count the nesting birds along established migratory routes. This survey, called the Breeding Bird Survey, has shown that 75 percent of the neotropical migrant bird species decreased in population between 1978 and 1987. Both woodland and grassland species are in trouble. Radar studies of the birds migrating over the Gulf of Mexico also reveal that the numbers are declining, perhaps by as much as 50 percent in the last thirty years.

Why are there fewer and fewer birds? There are several reasons, and most of them have to do with things people do.

Homelessness

The chief reason for the decline in bird populations is the destruction of bird habitat—the places where birds live and breed. Places where they stop over to rest and feed during their long journey of migration are important, too. The destruction of tropical rain forests, the birds' major wintering grounds, is without a doubt a major factor. Birds may leave their homes in the rain forest, fly thousands of miles to North America to breed, and then make the long journey south again, only to find their rain forest home is gone. If they go to another forest and try to live there, they probably won't survive. There's very little room for bird "refugees" in other forests, because they are filled with birds who already live there.

Fragmented Habitat

For a long time, people blamed the birds' decline entirely on the destruction of tropical rain forests. But it turns out, that is only part of the problem. Habitat destruction in the United States and Canada is a major factor, too. If something prevents neotropical migrant birds from successfully raising their young, their numbers quickly decline. There are fewer young birds to replace older ones that die during migration from being eaten by predators, from disease, or from other natural causes.

A lot of bird habitat in North America is destroyed outright to make room for houses, shopping malls, parking lots, landfills, and other construction. Worse still, the habitat that is left is not always suitable for the birds. Warbler species, for instance, are not very successful when they have to raise their young near the edges of forests, near roads, or near areas where all the trees have been cut down. That's because animals that eat eggs and baby birds are more common in these places. The predators include raccoons, domestic cats, bluejays, and crows.

The Egg Switchers

Forest edges are also home to cowbirds, which are called nest parasites. They are called parasites because, instead of building their own nests, they sneak their eggs into the nests of other birds. Sometimes cowbirds even throw out one or more of the eggs already in a nest! But even if all the host birds' eggs remain in the nest, the parent birds usually end up raising cowbirds instead of their own young. That's because cowbird eggs usually hatch first and the babies grow quickly. These bigger babies get more food than the other nestlings, and the smaller, weaker babies usually die or are pushed out of the nest.

Nest parasites such as cowbirds, as well as predator birds such as bluejays, threaten many bird species. To save the Kirtland's warbler, an endangered bird species, biologists have had to trap and remove cowbirds and bluejays from areas where the warblers nest.

Sharing and Caring

Today, people in South America, Central America, North America, and the Caribbean islands are banding together to save the birds they share. A program called Partners in Flight is helping coordinate their efforts.

Partners in Flight is run by the National Fish and Wildlife Foundation, an agency that is partly funded by the United States government. Partners in Flight helps other organizations carry out their work. These "partners" include the National Audubon Society, the Colorado Bird Observatory, and the Conservacion Manejo de Bosques Tropicales de Costa Rica. (Conservation Management of Tropical Forests of Costa Rica)

These groups identify what areas are critical to neotropical migrant birds and then take steps to preserve those areas. They buy land and help others buy land to set aside for bird habitat. They work with communities to help them benefit from the land without destroying bird habitat. They publish and distribute brochures to teach people about wildlife. They give workshops for park and nature preserve managers on how to better manage land so birds can survive.

Binocs for Birds

ndian parakeet

Birder's Exchange is another organization that is helping protect and conserve neotropical migrants. Many scientists, naturalists, park rangers, and educators in Central America, South America, and the Caribbean do not have money to purchase binoculars, books, nets, and other equipment they need. Without this equipment, they cannot properly partrol parks, study bird populations, or teach children and other visitors about nature. To solve this problem, the Manomet Bird Observatory of Massachusetts set up the Birder's Exchange. Through the program, people in the United States and Canada donate new and used binoculars, spotting scopes, cameras, lenses, tents, backpacks, field guides, and other equipment to needy bird conservationists in other countries.

Through Partners in Flight, Birder's Exchange, and many other programs, people in North, South, and Central America are banding together for a common goal: to save the birds. These efforts help people understand and care about tropical rain forests, even if they never visit one. With all these people working together, birds *and* tropical rain forests have a much better chance of survival.

For More Information

For information on Partners in Flight, contact:

National Fish and Wildlife Foundation
1120 Connecticut Avenue, N.W., Suite 900
Washington, DC 20036
U.S.A.
Phone: 1-202-857-0166
Fax: 1-202-857-0162
E-mail: Info@nfwf.org

For information on how you or your class can donate equipment to bird conservation in other countries, contact:

Birder's Exchange
Manomet Observatory
P.O. Box 1770
81 State Point Road
Manomet, MA 02345
U.S.A.
Phone: 1-508-224-6521
Fax: 1-508-224-9220

A booklet called the *Citizen's Guide to Migratory Bird Conservation* has a lot of information on how you can help neotropical migrant birds and birds in general. To get a copy, send $5.00 for one copy, or $2.00 each for five or more copies, to:

Cornell Lab of Ornithology
159 Sapsucker Woods Road
Ithaca, NY 14850
U.S.A.
Phone: 1-607-254-2473

KIDS SAVED IT!

Chris Wille

The roar of a howler monkey boomed through the treetops. Down below, four kids stopped walking and looked up. But the jungle was too dark and thick with leaves for them to see anything. Henri tried to copy the monkey's call. But his yell sounded more like a small hoot than a howl.

"No question who's king of *this* jungle," Cynthia said with a little chuckle.

Henri, Cynthia, Kevin, and Evelyn were exploring a tropical rain forest. They were in the mountains of Costa Rica, a small country in Central America. The kids weren't afraid of getting lost. The trail they were on was easy to follow, and they knew

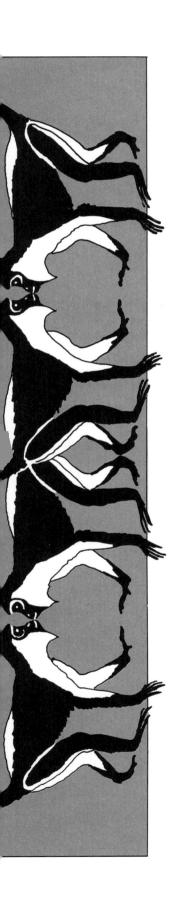

this forest like their own backyard. In fact, it *was* their backyard. They lived in Monteverde (MON-tay-VAIRday), a small village surrounded by deep rain forest.

The four kids moved on down the trail, looking here and there for the next discovery. They were glad to live in a place so full of incredible plants and animals.

There were so many sights, sounds, and smells in the forest that the four kids never got bored. There was always a new adventure, always a new surprise. But this rain forest was special in another way—it had been saved forever by kids just like themselves!

A Gift from the Children

In 1987, a scientist who studies rain forests visited a school in Sweden. She told the kids that the forests were being cut down—to make lumber and to clear the land for farms and ranches. She also told them that rain forests are the homes of millions of kinds of plants and animals. (So many different kinds live there that we may never discover and name them all.)

One of the kids, nine-year-old Roland Tiensuu, cared very much about wildlife. So he wondered what he could do to help save it. Then he had a great idea. "Why can't we earn money to help buy a rain forest park?" he asked. The scientist answered, "You can." And his teacher and classmates said, "Let's do it!"

By putting on plays, recycling, working at small jobs, making and selling T-shirts, saving allowances, and asking people for donations, the Swedish kids raised a lot of money. They sent it to a group of scientists in Costa Rica, who bought 15 acres (6 ha) of rain forest. (One acre is about the size of a football field.)

Soon, kids from all over Sweden began raising money to buy more rain forest. The idea spread to the United States, Canada, England, and Japan. So far, thousands of kids have raised more than a million dollars!

The money is used to buy parts of the rain forest around Monteverde. A special preserve there has been named the International Children's Rainforest. More than 14,000 acres have already been saved. And the monkeys, birds, and other things living there are now protected.

The Search for a Golden Toad

Henri, Cynthia, Kevin, and Evelyn moved along slowly, watching for birds and other animals. But they were looking especially for a famous creature called the golden toad. They wanted to show one to a group of kids from the United States. These kids had helped raise money for the forest, and now they were coming to visit.

Golden toads live only in the forests around Monteverde. And what makes them so special is that the male is completely orange. But the toads are so rare that they are very hard to find. If the kids found one today, they'd know where to look for more when their visitors were there.

"Let's check down by the creek," Kevin suggested. They scrambled down the trail to a small jungle stream. The Children's Rainforest has lots of creeks because it rains there almost every day. Around 118 inches (3 m) of rain falls every year. (A forest in the eastern United States gets around 45 inches, so you can see why a rain forest is so wet!)

Suddenly Evelyn let out a whistle. "Look!" she said. The others followed Evelyn's finger as she pointed into the treetops. Peeking down at the kids were two furry mammals—an olingo (OL-ing-go) and a tamandua (TUH-mun-DWA).

But then the kids saw something else. It was a quetzal (ket-SUL)—one of the most beautiful birds in the world. The quetzal's back is as green as an emerald. Its belly is as red as a ruby. And a male's tail feathers may be three feet (1 m) long. In ancient times, Mayan Indians used quetzal tail feathers to decorate the crowns of their kings.

Henri was now leading the others along the stream bank. Suddenly Cynthia whispered, "Careful of that salamander!" Just ahead of Henri's foot was a sleek, long-tailed creature. It blinked its eyes once, then scurried away under some dead leaves. Henri popped his hands down over the leaves and came up with his wiggling prize. The other kids checked out the salamander before Henri let it go.

After walking a little bit farther, Kevin stopped suddenly. "Wow, look!" he shouted. Everyone peered at what seemed to be a gleaming gold nugget lying on the ground. "Can you believe it? A gold beetle!" Gold beetles are one of the most beautiful insects on earth. And they are so rare that scientists know very little about them.

On a Tapir's Trail

The kids watched the beetle until it scurried out of sight. Then Cynthia noticed something on the muddy ground in front of Henri. It was a weird, three-toed track. A big track. Something with feet as big as a horse's had been there. All four kids knew what it had to be—a tapir (TAY-pur).

The tapir is the biggest animal in this forest. Its closest cousins are rhinoceroses and horses. But it looks more like a huge, dark brown pig with an extra-long snout. Tapirs live deep in the forest. At night they roam along streams and wander into forest clearings to feed. The Children's Rainforest is one of the few places left in Central America where tapirs can be found.

Now it was time for the kids to think about going home. "Well," said Evelyn, "we didn't find a golden toad."

"No, but maybe we'll get real lucky and find one when our visitors are here," said Henri. "Anyway, we *did* find a gold beetle, so we'll know where to look later. And there will always be lots of other neat things for our visitors to see. That's what's so special about a rain forest—you may not find what you're looking for, but what you *do* find is just as good."

The four young explorers headed back to get ready for their guests. All around them, the insects buzzed, the frogs croaked, and the birds chirped and screeched. High overhead a howler monkey roared. Henri tried again to copy the monkey's call. And this time it answered back.

The kids looked at each other and grinned. To them, the monkey and all the other creatures of the forest were like friends. But even more than that, the animals were living proof of what kids can do to help save the world.

three-toed sloth

Bibliography Update

Note: A * at the end of a listing indicates that the book is a good source of rain forest pictures.

GENERAL REFERENCE BOOKS

The Enchanted Canopy by Andrew W. Mitchell (Macmillan, 1986) *

Jungle by Theresa Greenaway (Knopf, 1994) *

In the Rainforest: Report from a Strange, Beautiful, Imperiled World by Catherine Caufield (University of Chicago Press, 1986)

People of the Tropical Rain Forest edited by Julie Sloan Denslow and Christine Padoch (University of California Press in association with Smithsonian Institution Traveling Exhibition Service, 1988) *

The Primary Source: Tropical Forests and Our Future by Norman Myers (Norton, 1992)

The Rainforest Book: How You Can Save the World's Rainforests by Scott Lewis (Living Planet Press, 1990)

Saving the Tropical Forests by Judith Gradwohl and Russell Greenberg (Island Press, 1988)

Tropical Nature: Life and Death in the Rain Forests of Central and South America by Andrew Forsyth and Kenneth Miyata (Scribners, 1987)

Tropical Rainforest by Arnold Newman (Facts on File, 1990)

CHILDREN'S BOOKS

Antonio's Rain Forest by Anna Lewington (Carolrhoda, 1992). Intermediate and Advanced

At Home in the Rain Forest by Diane Willow (Charlesbridge, 1991). Primary

Bats, Bugs, and Biodiversity: Adventures in the Amazonian Rain Forest by Susan E. Goodman (Atheneum, 1995). Intermediate

Amazing Tropical Birds by Gerald Legg (Knopf, 1991). Intermediate *

The Great Kapok Tree by Lynne Cherry (Harcourt Brace, 1990). Primary and Intermediate

Inside the Amazing Amazon by Don Lessem (Crown, 1995). Advanced

Journey Through a Tropical Jungle by Adrian Forsyth (Simon & Schuster, 1989). Intermediate and Advanced *

Jungle by Theresa Greenaway (Knopf, 1994). All Ages *

The Jungle by Carroll R. Norden (Raintree, 1988). Primary and Intermediate

Jungles by Illa Podendorf (Childrens Press, 1982). Primary and Intermediate *

Jungles by Angela Wilkes (EDC, 1980). Intermediate

Living Treasure: Saving Earth's Threatened Biodiversity by Laurence Pringle (Morrow, 1991). Intermediate

Look Closer: Rain Forest (Dorling Kindersley, 1991). Intermediate *

Nature Hide & Seek: Jungles by John Norris Wood and Keven Dean (Knopf, 1987). All Ages *

Nature's Green Umbrella: Tropical Rain Forests by Gail Gibbons (Morrow, 1994). Intermediate

Rain Forest by Paul Sterry and Michael H. Robinson (Reader's Digest, 1992). All Ages

Rain Forest Nature Search: A Hands-On Guide for Nature Sleuths (Reader's Digest, 1992). Advanced

Ranger Rick's Science Spectacular: Rainforest, part of the Science Spectacular series (Newbridge Communications, 1993). Primary and Intermediate. Call 1-800-347-7829 to subscribe to the series.

What Do We Know About Rainforests? by Brian Knapp (Peter Bedrick Books, 1992). Intermediate and Advanced

Where the Forest Meets the Sea by Jeannie Baker (Scholastic, 1993). Primary

GAMES, KITS, AND PUZZLES

National Wildlife Federation Exploration Kit: Rain Forest (Intermediate) contains an educational wheel with information on rain forest animals, a puzzle, and a mini mobile of rain forest butterflies. Available in children's toy and book stores.

The Rain Forest Giant Floor Puzzle is 5 feet long. Frank Schaffer Publications. Primary

Rainforest Exploration Kit (Intermediate) contains a magnifier, compass, posters, puzzle, games, activities, and mobile. Available from:
National Wildlife Federaton
1-800-822-9919

Up Close Rain Forest Wildlife (Intermediate) contains a book, board game, poster, model, and puzzles. Available in book stores. (Reader's Digest)

VIDEOS, FILMSTRIPS, AND OTHER RESOURCES

Amazonia: A Celebration of Life (1993) (Advanced) is available from:
Landmark Media
3450 Slade Run Dr.
Falls Church, VA 22042
U.S.A.

The Jungle (1992) (Advanced) is available from:
Ambrose Video
1290 Ave. of the Americas, Ste. 2245
New York, NY 10104
U.S.A.

orangutan

Newbridge Communications
fax to: 212-455-5750
Ranger Rick's Science Spectacular
for grades 2–4

COMPUTER PROGRAMS AND ON-LINE RESOURCES

McGraw-Hill, Inc.
1-800-722-4726
Earthscape, an interactive field guide to endangered habitats, ninth grade and up

Destination: Rain Forest (Primary and Intermediate) is an interactive CD-ROM that allows children to create their own rain forest story books based on factual information. Integrates language arts, science, social studies, art, and music. (Edmark, 1995)

EE-Link contains numerous links to a wide variety of environmental topics including rain forests. Their Web site is at:
http://www.nceet.snre.umich.edu/

Rainforest Workshop Home Page was developed and is maintained by seventh-grade students at Marshall Middle School in Olympia, Washington. The page contains information and activities on rain forest mammals geared toward intermediate and advanced students. The Web site is at:
http://mh.osd.wednet.edu/

Zoo Guides: The Rainforest (Advanced) CD-ROM covers flora and fauna with information on conservation issues. Children can learn about the types of rain forests and their ecology, can view maps, and can learn about the people living in these regions. Animals and plants of the rain forests are highlighted. Children can view videos, take quizzes, and print out information. (REMedia, 1994)

Zurk's Rainforest Lab (Primary and Intermediate) is a CD-ROM that allows children to explore the levels of the rain forest and learn about plants and animals, sort animals by classification, make a photo album of observed animals, and put together pattern puzzles. The program switches easily between English, French, and Spanish and comes with a teacher's guide. (Soleil Software, 1994)

OTHER ACTIVITY SOURCES

Earth Force has a program, Pennies for the Planet, in which children collect money to benefit rain forests as well as other habitats. They also have a Rain Forest Rap sheet and other materials that encourage children of all ages to become involved in protecting the environment. Contact them at:
Earth Force
1501 Wilson Blvd., 12th Floor
Arlington, VA 22209
U.S.A.
(703) 243-7400
Or visit their Web site at:
http://www.earthforce.org/earthforce

National Geographic Society has a large selection of rain forest videos, filmstrips, software, and classroom materials:
Eye on the Environment: Rain Forests is a poster set containing three full-color posters and teacher's guide.
Rain Forests is part of the Earth's Endangered Environments filmstrip set or CD-ROM for intermediate and advanced students.
Really Wild Animals: Totally Tropical Rain Forest (Intermediate) and ***Rain Forest*** (Advanced) are two of the videos available.
STV: Rain Forest (Intermediate and Advanced) is an interactive videodisk.
For catalogs and more information, call:
1-800-368-2728

Rainforest for Children (1996) (Intermediate and Advanced) video series contains three titles:
• ***Animals of the Rainforest***
• ***People of the Rainforest***
• ***Plants of the Rainforest***
For information call:
Schlessinger Video Productions
1-800-843-3620

Spirits of the Rainforest (1993) (Advanced) For information write:
F.P. Video
c/o Discovery Channel
6360 Lapas Trail
Indianapolis, IN 46268
U.S.A.

Environmental Media offers various materials on the rain forest, including the video ***Two Worlds Touch*** (1991) (Advanced). Contact them at:
P.O. Box 99
Beaufort, SC 29901
U.S.A.
1-800-368-3382

Educational Insights
1-800-933-3277
Sticker books for kids ages 3 and up

EPI, Inc.
203-259-7637
Ranger Rick Exploration Kits
for ages 6-12

Earth Foundation offers a rain forest curriculum containing teacher's guide, video, posters, and activities. The curriculum comes in levels appropriate for all ages. Free. Call:
1-800-5MONKEY (1-800-566-6539)

Rainforest Action Network offers fact sheets, lists of resources, slide sets, and the publication *Rainforests Are Amazing*, a kid's action guide to helping preserve rain forests and the people living in them. Teachers can obtain one free copy of the kid's guide for their classrooms. They also offer Treasures of the Rainforest, a curriculum designed for advanced students that contains activities and projects. Call them at:
(415) 398-4404
or visit their Web page at:
http://www.ran.org/ran/

Bananas and Balsa, Quetzals and Quinine: A Rain Forest Unit for Science and Language Arts (Advanced) by Jean Pottle contains student activities and a teacher's guide. Available from:
J. Weston Walch
(207) 772-2846

Spotlight on Science: Rainforest (Intermediate and Advanced) is a kit containing 24 hands-on experiments and materials to conduct them. Teacher's guide included. From:
Learning Resources
1-800-222-3909

Vanishing Rain Forests Education Kit (Primary and Intermediate) contains a full-color poster, black and white poster, background information, and teacher's guide with several classroom activities. Also included is ***Rain Forest Rap***, a six-minute video extolling the beauty of the rain forest set to rap music. Available from:
World Wildlife Fund Publications
P.O. Box 4866 Hampden Post Office
Baltimore, MD 21211
U.S.A.
(410) 516-6951

WHERE TO GET MORE INFORMATION

- college and university departments of natural resources, biology, botany, and zoology
- organizations working to protect tropical rain forests (for a partial list, see page 54)
- zoos, museums, and botanical gardens with rain forest exhibits (see list on page 69)

Internet Address Disclaimer
The Internet information provided here was correct, to the best of our knowledge, at the time of publication. It is important to remember, however, the dynamic nature of the Internet. Resources that are free and publicly available one day may require a fee or restrict access the next, and the location of items may change as menus and homepages are reorganized.

leopard cat